Innovative Strategy Making in Higher Education

Innovative Strategy Making in Higher Education

Mario C. Martinez

Mimi Wolverton

INFORMATION AGE PUBLISHING, INC.
Charlotte, NC • www.infoagepub.com

Library of Congress Cataloging-in-Publication Data

Martinez, Mario, 1967-
  Innovative strategy making in higher education / Mario C. Martinez, Mimi
Wolverton.
      p. cm.
  Includes bibliographical references and index.
  ISBN 978-1-60752-049-8 (pbk.) – ISBN 978-1-60752-050-4 (hardcover)
1. Public universities and colleges–United States–Administration. 2.
Education, Higher–United States–Planning. 3. Strategic planning–United
States. I. Wolverton, Mimi. II. Title.
  LB2341.M293 2009
  378.1'07–dc22

                                                              2008055681

Printed in the United States of America

CONTENTS

ACKNOWLEDGMENTS

Several years ago we felt compelled to write a book on strategy for higher education leaders. We had both conducted research on organizations and individual leaders within higher education and found many sterling examples of strategy in action. We also found examples of leaders and organizations clinging to strategic processes that have somewhat lost their luster. Some leaders unconsciously took action with little regard to systematic strategy making. Others followed no clear strategy or direction.

Our observations and discoveries required access. We thank the many higher education leaders who gave us access to their wisdom and their organizations over the years, particularly Bob McCabe, Lattie Coor, Tad Perry, and Larry Penley. The business college at San Diego State University provided a teaching opportunity for a summer course in strategy, which was the perfect vehicle to deepen our thinking about how strategy might more systematically apply to organizations in the higher education industry. Dr. Michael Cunningham specifically arranged this opportunity, and for that we are grateful. We also wish to thank George Johnson, from Information Age Publishing. George and his team have been easy to work with and have encouraged us from the start.

PREFACE

Globally, higher education in the United States constitutes a powerhouse industry. Some institutions in the U.S. have been functioning and thriving since the 1600s; others have evolved and come to full maturity since the 1970s, meeting the new and changing needs of the markets they serve. Throughout the eras of growth and change in higher education, there have been opportunities and challenges. At the same time, institutions—particularly public ones—have had to balance competing demands from multiple constituencies. The need for effective strategy making is critical for public colleges and universities, yet there remains a curious absence of systematic strategy analysis in this sector.

This book primarily focuses on strategy making for public colleges and universities. The chapters draw heavily on examples from public higher education to illustrate the fundamental axioms of strategy making while recognizing the many institutional types that populate the entire industry. There are, of course, many notable strategy lessons from private institutions of higher education as well, and we highlight them where applicable and appropriate. Strategy as applied to organizations has long been affiliated with business and government organizations, so we very explicitly refer to examples and references from this source also—once again, as long as there exist applications or lessons for public higher education.

Our modern-day view of strategy really began in the 1950s. Large corporations and government agencies adopted budgetary planning and control models. During this time, budgeting for operating and capital expenses translated into coordination and control, from a financial perspective. Corporate planning, and more specifically strategic planning, gained momen-

Innovative Strategy Making in Higher Education, pages ix–xiii
Copyright © 2009 by Information Age Publishing

tum in the 1960s and early '70s. Strategic planning, as a formal strategy tool, soon found its way into colleges and universities. It was really during this period that the very term strategy became a common part of organizational lexicon.

Strategies that focused on competitors and how one's organization was positioned within the industry environment characterized the 1980s and '90s. Porter's (1980) impact on the field of strategy took full root during this era of strategy, as organizations around the world examined their industries and how they ranked within them. At the same time, many prominent consulting organizations, such as the Boston Consulting Group, derived clever and useful tools to strategically help organizations think about their portfolio of products or services and how they were positioned in the industry. From a strategy perspective, this enabled the massive conglomerate corporations of the day, exemplified by the General Electric (GE) model, to manage its many different businesses. GE's portfolio of businesses ranged from light bulbs to airplane engines, but the complexities of managing across such divergent products and services produced many challenges. Business leaders were soon balancing focus with diversity, as they attempted to find the right mixture of products and services to gain a competitive edge. Explicit consideration of joint ventures and strategic alliances also marked the time, as organizations searched for partners with whom they could combine forces to produce mutually beneficial results.

The strategy lessons of the '80s and '90s largely passed higher education by, with little consideration or notice. Higher education institutions tended to stay with the strategic planning models to which they had grown accustomed. In retrospect, competitive analysis and portfolio management probably held little appeal for colleges and universities because, on the face, they did little to illuminate the student growth and public good goals so central to the core of institutional missions. But institutions do have a complex mixture of services they offer, and the management of the nation's largest universities means that presidents are running multibillion dollar conglomerate businesses. In addition, institutions today make no secret of competing for students, faculty, and research dollars. Given this context, there is little doubt that the lessons of competitive strategy do hold some instruction for higher education—or at least they merit consideration.

Strategic planning and competitive strategy both contributed to the maturation of strategy as a field, but together or individually they cannot substitute for a comprehensive strategy. The complex interaction of variables in and outside the organization means that strategy must be more dynamic and responsive. For these reasons, innovation has now emerged as a premier strategy. The concept of innovation is somewhat diffuse and not easily defined, yet it is precisely because of the creativity involved in strategic innovation that new tools, actions, and inventions have arisen on the strategy scene over the last decade.

Innovation can be the purposeful creation of an entirely new service or product, based on the ingenuity, knowledge, and experience of those tasked with strategy. Innovation may involve tapping new markets based on a strategy that combines elements of fiscal and strategic planning, positioning and competitive strategy. Innovation also might require applying new strategic tools that help leaders simultaneously create new products and services and open new markets.

Strategy itself is multidimensional and can be defined in many different ways. There are common threads, however. Strategy involves the planning and analysis that allow an organization to fulfill its purpose and reach its goals. The very notion that planning and analysis are necessary implies that organizations operate in an environment that is, to some extent, unknown, unpredictable, or changing in such a way that the modus operandi no longer serves to ensure survival or progress. Public higher education exists in such an environment. No one denies that funding challenges, the emergence of for-profit and international institutions, technological advancements, and changing student expectations have altered the landscape inhabited by public colleges and universities.

If public institutions are among those organizations that assume the future will simply be a reflection of the past, they will be hard hit by the changing realities in a dynamic world that is full of both challenge and opportunity. Those institutions that examine emerging trends and look at their own purpose and function while asking how tomorrow might differ from today will be the successes of the future. Here, then, is where strategy comes into play. Strategy is an invaluable tool that organizational leaders and the people who work within them can use (or at least consider) to proactively contribute to their own sustainability and organizational health.

In this book, we detail the various strategic tools that have had an impact on organizational strategy throughout the years. Each of the strategy tools is reviewed and applied to higher education. Chapter 1 sets the stage for the rest of the book. It provides a brief look at the general topic of strategy and explores its application to higher education. In this chapter, we expand on some of the changes facing higher education leaders and present a strategy framework for the remaining chapters.

Chapter 2 examines strategic planning in concept and practice. The application of this tool has a rich history in higher education, and there is little question that many of the building blocks of strategic planning can inform a more comprehensive organizational strategy. Chapter 3 is an application chapter for strategic planning, and in it we provide real world examples of strategic planning and suggest a template to enhance the strategic planning process. We do not, however, promote the notion that a more robust strategic planning process can ever substitute for a comprehensive strategy approach. A primary danger for colleges and universities that depend solely on strategic planning is that it can become an end in and of itself, a plan that affords little maneuverability in response to the rapid changes that face the industry.

Chapters 4 and 5 discuss and apply industry analysis to higher education. Higher education as an industry was once equated with four-year universities, but today that view is narrow and limiting. The term "postsecondary" education, which includes two-year and proprietary institutions, may have even run its course. We make the case that from a strategic perspective the postsecondary education industry has morphed into a global postsecondary education and training industry. Today, individuals seeking new and additional learning opportunities look for experiences tailored to their specific needs and preferences. They can gain such intellectual capital at corporate universities, in one-day seminars, at for-profit universities and, of course, through traditional colleges and universities. An industry analysis uncovers the forces and factors that shape the new industry in which more traditional public colleges and universities now exist.

Chapters 6 and 7 are in some ways extensions of Chapters 4 and 5. Both of these chapters speak to specific competitive strategies that organizations use to survive and thrive. The strategies of differentiation, focus, and cost leadership have long been part and parcel of higher education strategy, albeit often unconsciously exercised and seldom named as such. Higher education-related examples of the three strategies form the crux of Chapter 6, while Chapter 7 addresses vertical and horizontal integration strategies. Vertical integration, as used in the book, primarily refers to institutional strategies that attempt to control organizational inputs or outputs, many of which were formerly completed through the activities of other people or organizations; horizontal integration primarily refers to growth by expansion.

Chapter 8 introduces a relatively new strategy tool known as the strategy canvas. This innovative tool, popularized by Kim and Mauborgne (2005), lets the astute leader examine strategic possibilities across industries to create new services and open new markets. Fundamentally, the technique points to opportunity. Although much of the work and commentary on strategy canvassing explains success after the fact, the tool provides insight into the evolution of higher education as an industry and can be applied at the institution, college, department, or even program level with a bit of creativity. As with all new tools, applications surface over time. The value of introducing this tool is that practitioners are free to use it in new and creative ways rather than being limited to tradition.

Innovation as a formal concept is the subject of Chapter 9. Innovative strategy making can draw on new tools (e.g., strategy canvassing) and old tools (strategic planning and competitive analysis), combining them in unique ways to help strategists capitalize on opportunities. In this chapter, we provide guidelines to encourage innovation. Perhaps most important, we illustrate innovation in action by highlighting examples of public colleges and universities that have turned this abstract concept into reality.

Chapter 10 ends the volume with an emphasis on leadership. Leadership and strategy are two sides of the same coin. One does not work without the other. Leaders of public colleges and universities face unique challenges in formulating strategy because of the many stakeholders who make different demands and hold competing values and interests. Once again, however, there are numerous higher education examples of bold leaders who capably executed strategy, skillfully balanced constituent interests, and moved their institutions or entire systems to success.

As a whole, this book suggests that business as usual in public higher education will no longer work. There are simply too many changes around and within colleges and universities to assume that yesterday's existence guarantee tomorrow's. The time is ripe to discuss strategy and how it pertains to public higher education—at the institution, college, department, and program levels. Those colleges and universities that do not adopt new strategies or seek to at least consider the many changes that are sweeping the industry face probable costs that include weakening political and fiscal support; erosion of faculty morale and student enthusiasm; and, in the most extreme case, the closing of their doors. The costs of ignoring strategy are high, its benefits limitless.

Mario Martinez
Mimi Wolverton
December 2008

CHAPTER 1

THE NEW IMPERATIVE
FOR STRATEGY MAKING

Compared to business organizations, American colleges and universities have, in many respects, been remarkably stable fixtures on the national landscape. Corporations that were major players in their industries just twenty years ago no longer exist. Ken Olsen founded Digital Equipment Corporation (DEC) in 1957 and turned it into a true pioneer in the computer industry. But in the 1990s, DEC struggled badly and began selling off businesses that were bleeding red ink. DEC—or what was left of it—was eventually bought by Compaq in 1998, which was, in turn, purchased by Hewlett-Packard in 2002. People Express Airline started in 1981 and in two years was the fastest growing airline in the country, with its signature low-cost fares and limited service. In 1985, two years after its peak, the airline started to crumble due to overexpansion, sharp competition, and overwhelmed operations. The company, unable to properly manage its growth, was eventually taken over by Continental Airlines in 1987. Business books are filled with hundreds of other examples of large companies that died or languished so badly that they were acquired by other organizations.

In contrast to these dramatic examples of demise, the longevity of higher education institutions, from Harvard in 1636 to the relatively recent establishment of the University of Nevada, Las Vegas in 1957, is notable. The stability of institutions of higher education, however, masks the many changes that occur within the higher education industry. Experts disagree

Innovative Strategy Making in Higher Education, pages 1–9
Copyright © 2009 by Information Age Publishing
All rights of reproduction in any form reserved.

as to whether changes are imposed on colleges and universities or created from within them, but the end result is that change happens. For the past 20 years or so, dramatic changes in the higher education industry have shut programs and threatened entire institutions. The changes range from unpredictable state funding to shifting student attitudes.

In the late 1980s and early 1990s, observers began to emphasize the changing revenue structure of public universities, as state funding consistently and continuously comprised a smaller portion of institutional operating budgets. This ongoing pattern has made it necessary for universities to increase tuition levels and look for outside funding sources, especially from private businesses and well-heeled donors.

Even in instances where state funding will remain strong, there is no guarantee that the manner in which that funding occurs will stay the same. Institutions may prefer direct appropriations to pay for operational costs, but policy makers often have different ideas. For instance, many states increasingly favor an approach that provides aid to students rather than institutions, thus creating a more market-driven higher education industry. Recent developments in the state of Colorado have in principle replaced all direct appropriations to public institutions, instead putting the money in "vouchers" or "stipends" to be spent by students at institutions of their choice. Such alterations in the level and manner of funding have ramifications for college and university leaders and are salient factors when it comes to institutional strategy making.

Social and demographic shifts continue to occur as well, and corresponding adaptations to accommodate emerging student populations in colleges and universities have appeared across a range of institutions. The "Net generation" of students is pressing institutions and professors to examine pedagogy and how technology (beyond the ubiquitous slide show) can be used to promote learning. As a result, some institutions offer downloadable lectures, which free students from the confines of time and place that are imposed on them by more traditional colleges and universities. Similarly, doctoral programs increasingly offer night and weekend courses to meet the needs of working students—a necessity driven by competition for students from private, for-profit providers that have no attachment to traditional daytime offerings.

Rethinking course and program offerings has always been a part of higher education, but today the issue cuts deeper to decisions about how to manage emerging programs and what to do about those that are struggling. Consider the nascent field of Homeland Security compared with computer science. The federal government has given universities millions of dollars to develop programs and degrees in homeland security, and these universities must now answer crucial questions: Under which college should such programs be located? What should the curriculum look like? How much actual student demand exists for graduate degrees in homeland security? How can demand be created? What is the appropriate background for a qualified faculty member in such a program?

On the opposite side of the spectrum lies computer science. As a major, computer science in U.S. institutions has lost currency. In an increasingly global and economically driven world, countries like India and China provide equivalent pools of computer science talent. Companies regularly outsource technology work to India and pay a fraction of what it would cost to employ the services of workers in the U.S. labor market. India and China increasingly have the capacity and knowledge to train their own labor markets as well, meaning that institutions in these countries directly compete with U.S. universities for students. In turn, Chinese and Indian students graduate and compete with American graduates for the right to provide expertise and service to employers.

Computer science is not the only area in which change is causing colleges and universities to reconsider curriculum content or entire programs. Companies such as Hewlett-Packard look to the Indias of the world to strategically outsource basic marketing work so that the remaining core of U.S. employees can concentrate on higher level, strategic marketing activities. Such moves mean that the college graduate looking for entry-level marketing work no longer has the palette of employment options that were once available since entry-level tasks are being farmed out to workers in other countries. Such shifts carry implications for how colleges and universities develop and deliver program curriculum if graduates are to remain competitive.

In sum, American colleges and universities face many challenges: changing revenue sources and mix; increasing pressure to raise external monies; increased competition by private, proprietary, international, and corporate educational sources; changing demographics, which alter the nature of demand; and an evolving global economy, which increases the demand for some majors and suppresses it for others. All of these imperatives (and many more) underscore the need for higher education leaders to systematically and formally integrate innovative strategy making tools into their decision calculus.

MOVING FROM STRATEGIC PLANNING TO INNOVATIVE STRATEGY MAKING

No one in today's environment denies that colleges and universities must have a strategy for the future. Beginning in the 1970s, public colleges and universities across the country adopted strategic planning, a classic business tool, as a way to move toward that future. And, although strategic planning has lost its luster in many business organizations, it remains a fixture on virtually every college campus in America. The ample writings on strategic planning within the field of higher education, ranging from the conceptual (Peterson, Dill, Mets, & Associates, 1997) to step-by-step instructions on completing the process (Rowley, Lujan, & Dolence, 1997), attest to this fact. However, a common misconception held by too many higher education leaders is that strategic planning and strategy are synonymous. As a consequence, institutionalization of strategic planning in American colleges and universities has come at the expense of using new strategy concepts and tools, which can complement and in some instances replace the sacrosanct strategic planning process.

As early as 1979, Jelinek (1979) criticized the machine-like exercise of strategic planning at Texas Instruments and questioned whether innovation could be institutionalized through this process. Successful practitioners also have been leery of organizational dependence on strategic planning. Jack Welch, the legendary, former CEO of General Electric, cautions against the "scenario planning" and the "scientific approach" to strategy taught in business schools and practiced in too many organizations. In its place, he advocates a more creative system of planning (Welch & Welch, 2005). McFarland (2008) has said that traditional strategic planning is dead and that leaders who fail to see the difference between strategy and strategic planning are unlikely to harness the true power of creativity and innovation. Part of McFarland's assault on strategic planning lies in its failure to account for and adapt to rapid change. The political, economic, social, and technological shifts that confront every public college and university today certainly qualify as rapid change and signal a need to reexamine strategy making in higher education.

Table 1 suggests a comprehensive strategy-making schema. This schema builds on practices already in place on most college and university campuses and introduces strategy-making endeavors that are more interpretive in nature into the conventional higher education planning rubric. Table 1 highlights tools that colleges and universities will increasingly need to consider if they hope to be industry leaders, capitalizing on changes within the industry instead of falling victim to them.

Traditional Analysis

In today's higher education environment, institutions that embrace strategic planning exercise two aspects of traditional analysis to arrive at a strategic plan: organizational analysis and environmental analysis. Organizational analysis provides a rational backdrop for a more politically charged environmental analysis. A key assumption of organizational analysis is that

---

TABLE 1   Moving Toward Innovative Strategy Making

Traditional Analysis

Organizational:
- Mission, goals, objectives
- Internal resources and capabilities
- Organizational structures and systems
- Strengths and Weaknesses

Environmental:
- PEST (political, economic, social, technological)
- Opportunities and Threats

= *Strategic Plan*

Competitive Analysis
- Industry Analysis
- Competitive Strategies

= *Competitive Advantage*

Innovation
- Strategy Canvassing
- Innovative Entrepreneurialism
- Innovative Competitiveness
- Previous tools
- New tools

= *Innovative Strategy Making*

---

common goals exist and policies can be put in place to drive the desired institutional action necessary to achieve said goals. In reality, not everyone agrees with the stipulated goals, resources might or might not surface, and policies already in place very likely hamper the execution of prescribed actions.

The purpose of an organizational analysis is to build an internal assessment of an institution. It provides a logical starting point for strategy making because all organizations have access to their own documents, memos, and financials. Employees, suppliers, and consumers are usually available for input and feedback as well. Critical analysis of all of these sources can help a university assess its resources and capabilities, its strengths and weaknesses, and the appropriateness of its structures and systems. Review of an institution's mission, goals, and objectives can provide a retrospective evaluation of organizational effectiveness.

Environmental analysis has typically been distinguished from an organizational analysis. While an organizational analysis looks at the inside workings of the organization, an environmental analysis looks at factors outside of the organization which are difficult if not impossible to control. In truth, an organization and its environment cannot be completely separated because the environment informs the internal workings of the organization.

For example, contingency planning, a form of strategic planning, examines organization/environment compatibility (Morgan, 2006) as does organizational cultural analysis (Kotter & Haskett, 1992). A comprehensive environmental analysis aids decision makers in gauging whether the existing mission, goals, objectives, structures, and systems need revision.

An environmental analysis can also help leaders assess whether resources and capabilities should be redirected toward different ends. Most environmental analyses in higher education planning documents focus primarily on opportunities and threats, giving cursory attention to political, economic, social, and technological factors (PEST analysis), which impinge on and color organizational options. The opportunities and threats are usually predicated on decision maker or committee experiences, and, in the best cases, are considered simultaneously with the organizational analysis. Combined, organizational and environmental analyses have traditionally been the basis of strategic planning, and together they set forth the parameters under which an institution can adapt to, or at least, coexist with its environment.

Competitive Analysis

Competitive analysis moves beyond strategic planning. Although it is briefly mentioned in higher education writings, it is not explored to the extent to which it has been studied and scrutinized in the business and public administration literatures. Competitive analysis tells a college or university more about its environment than does an environmental scan because it provides information about competitors, suppliers, and current and potential clientele. Popularized by Porter (1980), this analysis of the industry's structure is primarily descriptive but offers useful insights that inform subsequent strategy. At the very least, through an industry analysis, strategists gain a view of and appreciation for the entire industry in which their organizations operate.

An industry analysis is the starting point of competitive analysis, which is a systematic review of industry forces. Industry analysis has been heavily used in the business and government arenas, from emergency services (Pines, 2006) to retail clothing (Fratto, Jones, & Cassill, 2006), but it is unusual to find an explicit industry analysis of Porter's five forces (buyers, suppliers, substitutes, new entrants, and intensity of rivalry) in higher education planning or strategy documents.

The structure of higher education as an industry, examined through an industry analysis, has clear implications for strategy making in colleges and universities. The strategy for a public university located in a state where public institutions enroll 95% of the student population (monopoly) will be different from a strategy for an institution that operates next to a number of well-known private universities (closer to perfect competition). Many universities in the West, for instance, operate in the former situation, while public universities located along the East Coast area operate in the latter. An institution that sketches a profile of students and the presence of different institutional types (two of higher education's industry forces) is certainly positioned to make more informed strategic choices than one that does not.

Strategy choices, in competitive analysis, are largely informed by Porter's work on establishing a competitive advantage. His generic strategies suggest that an organization can compete on cost, focus on a particular niche market, or provide something unique to differentiate a service offering. In the traditional higher and postsecondary industry, community colleges draw a substantial number of students because they are affordable, relative to other alternatives. Thus, one competitive advantage of the community college is based on the generic strategy of cost advantage. World-renowned institutions, such as Stanford, differentiate themselves based on quality, which is achieved through leading faculty, the production of research, and the type of students they attract. Institutions like the Colorado School of Mines seek a narrow market niche and focus their efforts on technical and scientific disciplines. Clearly, competitive analysis is a tool to help organizations more deeply understand their environment and the players comprising that environment so that the ultimate strategies they craft maximize the opportunity for gain in a competitive world.

Innovation

Vision and goals are captured in the strategic planning process, but the creativity and flexibility required to realize the vision and actually move forward might in fact require new tools, new ideas, and new ways of doing things. True innovation demands a level of thinking and learning that encourages strategists to draw on various tools and experiences and discourages them from being content with simply replicating the past. In a changing world, it may in fact be dangerous to believe that replicating past strategies will lead to future success, something Christensen (1997) has dubbed the innovator's dilemma.

Although competitive analysis creates a comprehensive picture of the industry in which one exists, innovation demands that we move beyond studying the competition. Indeed, one criticism of competitive analysis is that sole dependence on it reduces the organization to an endless game of chasing the competition. In contrast, innovation opens up new possibilities.

Innovative organizations build on traditional and competitive analyses but do not assume that these methods are sufficient to create a comprehensive, dynamic strategy. There are always new and emerging tools to help decision makers see new things or old things in new ways. The strategy canvas is an example of such a tool (Chapter 8). A strategy canvas provides a powerful visual of combinations of factors that make organizations from different industries successful (Kim & Mauborgne, 2005). It points to possibilities where new strategies might emerge. Strategy canvassing requires knowledge of the competition inside and outside the industry, but the creativity and innovation involved in going through the canvassing process moves beyond competitive analysis.

Innovation is not a prescribed, step-by-step process. Opportunity takes different forms, and the strategies that best position an organization to capitalize on it are almost always customized to fit the situation. Some colleges and universities might learn from the success of a competitor and duplicate the activity that led to that success. If the institution that duplicates the activity has more capability and infrastructure than the originator, then the duplicator will more than likely gain market share. In Table 1, this type of innovation is referred to as competitive innovation. Entrepreneurial innovation is a different approach. Colleges and universities are seedbeds of creativity, and often the innovation that emerges is new and unique. The resulting strategic advantage, which might draw more students, higher quality faculty, or additional research dollars, can be attributed to the institution's entrepreneurial innovation.

CLOSING COMMENTS

Every tool that is used in the strategy-making process has its strengths and weaknesses. Some tools describe the world in which colleges and universities live, but they don't provide information that assists departments in making actual choices about creating new degree programs or retiring existing ones. Other tools, such as strategy canvassing, not only describe organizational and industry environments, but suggest strategy by pointing organizations in a specific direction. The underutilization of strategy tools in higher education is, at least partially, due to a reluctance to adopt the language and tools of business. As change continues to impinge upon old ways of operating, colleges and universities will need to consider new tools and ideas if they are to be successful in the future, regardless of their origin.

Effective innovative strategy making does not discount the foundations of strategy that have been laid by traditional and competitive analysis techniques. The results of those techniques have their place, and they can be properly integrated into a comprehensive strategy. But innovation as strategy is the way to the future. In today's world, where demographic, technological, economic, and political changes consistently occur at both the local and global levels, those leaders and decision makers who rely exclusively on traditional and competitive analysis will produce less than optimal strategies for their colleges and universities. It is the innovative strategy maker's institution that will emerge as the most viable.

In this book, we take lessons from the past, combine them with the experiences of a select group of strategy-making pioneers, and incorporate them into a framework for future strategy making. As such, we begin with a comprehensive examination of strategic planning in higher education in the next chapter, followed by in depth discussions of competitive analysis and then innovation. We recognize that strategies do not magically appear. Arriving at them takes hard work; executing them requires insight, foresight, fortitude, perseverance, and guidance. Given this reality, the last chapter focuses on leadership, a key ingredient of innovative strategy making.

CHAPTER 2

THE COSTS AND BENEFITS
OF STRATEGIC PLANNING

Strategic planning, long synonymous with strategy, gained popularity in the private sector in the 1960s, as organizations looked for new ideas to replace the budgeting, planning, and control systems of the 1950s (Grant, 2005). Strategic planning maintained a central place in organizational life throughout the 1980s, although many leaders and observers began to question its value.

Lawler (2006, p. 547) points out that organizations are increasingly abandoning strategic planning efforts because it simply has not produced the results that justify its costs. Mintzberg's (1994) earlier assessment was harsher, indicating that even the term strategic planning is an oxymoron. He contends that strategy making is about creativity and gaining competitive advantage, whereas planning is about analysis and rationalization. Strategic planning relies on hierarchy, which is quite possibly another weakness of the approach given today's changing technological environment. Hierarchy often blunts creativity and adaptability. Tapscott and Williams (2006) write to this very point, and they give perhaps the most devastating commentary on organizations that hold on to past practices for security, stating that the old hierarchical ways of organizing work and innovation do not afford the level of creativity and agility that organization's need to be competitive (p. 31).

Innovative Strategy Making in Higher Education, pages 11–23
Copyright © 2009 by Information Age Publishing
11

Indeed, the consensus by authors who address strategy seems to be that strategic planning is no longer a valuable strategy-making tool. Yet, despite the persuasive arguments that strategic planning is an outmoded practice, most colleges and universities still use it as their primary strategy tool. Although a disproportionate number of colleges and universities mistakenly use strategic planning as their only strategy tool, strategic planning and its various components still hold potential value. In addition, new strategy tools build on the lessons of old ones, and many of the concepts (missions, goals, etc.) embedded in strategic planning form the foundation for strategy making in general. The innovative strategy maker does not completely discount any tool, past or present, and properly discerns when different tools apply to different situations.

AN HISTORICAL SNAPSHOT OF STRATEGIC PLANNING IN HIGHER EDUCATION

Traditional strategic planning explores options available to an institution and limits choices to those that maximize value and deal best with environmental conditions. Strategic planning has persisted in the academy largely because it is a rational process well suited to the hierarchical decision making processes found within its administrative structures. The cornerstone of any viable strategic planning effort rests on the concepts of reasonableness, efficiency, and effective use of organizational resources, all of which epitomize the concept of rationality and fit well with the Enlightenment philosophies upon which universities and colleges are built.

In practice, strategic planning can and has been used to rationalize management decisions, both good and bad. It gained significant momentum in higher education in the 1970s because it defined a systematic process for strategy making in a time of fiscal uncertainty. In 1972, Carnegie Mellon University (CMU) (an early strategic planning adopter in higher education) faced financial adversity brought on by successive years of sizable operating budget deficits. As Richard Cyert took over the presidency, the institution was floundering for lack of direction. Cyert set a three-pronged strategic plan in place to gain control of financial management, encourage individual initiative in building distinctive programs, and move CMU to national prominence, all of which the institution accomplished (Gilley, Fulmer, & Reithlingshoefer, 1986; Keller, 1983). Here, then, is a sterling example of how strategic planning helped transform an institution.

Institutions have also used strategic planning to justify decisions that seem rational but in fact are intended to preserve institutional choices, no matter the consequences. In the 1980s, the University of Tennessee at Knoxville (UTK) took this tack in its strategic planning initiative when it reduced enrollment and raised admission standards. The main objective was to preserve quality and at the same time encourage students who exhibited little chance of academic success to seek remedial help elsewhere (Gilley et al., 1986). The driving force behind this particular initiative came from the state's promise of more money if the university could demonstrate significant cognitive growth in its undergraduates. UTK's planning clearly identified student performance as a priority, but its primary underlying focus was on making the university more successful and monetarily better off. It achieved this task by simply limiting access to students who demonstrated higher cognitive abilities in the first place—a strategy that precluded the necessity of rethinking UTK's learning environment and the overall delivery of its programs.

CLASSIC STRATEGIC PLANNING

Strategic planning is a disciplined effort to produce fundamental decisions and actions that shape and guide what an organization is, what it does, and why it does it (Quinn, Mintzberg, & James, 1988; Shirley, 1988). Much of the value of engaging in strategic planning lies in the very process of producing the plan. Through this process, institutions gain a better understanding of whom they are and of the context in which they function. Based on this knowledge, strategic plans become mechanisms for prioritizing activities and ensuring that adequate resources are available to meet set goals. Proponents of strategic planning strive to place the organization in a distinctive and thus defendable position (Keller, 1983). In effect, strategic planning becomes a continuous process of effectively relating organizational objectives and resources to opportunities in the environment. These plans for the future, grounded in patterns of the past, look at the chain of cause and effect consequences of actual or intended decisions over time (Mintzberg, 1989).

Classic strategic planning consists of several components that, in theory, together constitute the strategy of the organization and answer what an organization is, what it does, and why it does it. The components of strategic planning include the mission, vision, analyzing the organization and its environment, and creating goals, objectives, and performance measures.

The Mission and Vision

The starting point in any strategic planning process is creating a vision and mission statements to determine the direction of the organization. The mission provides focus. The vision provides direction. All subsequent goals and performance measures in the plan tie directly back to the focus and promote movement in the prescribed direction. Ideally, the ordained mission and vision of the organization also drive budgetary decisions. A strategic planning process that is mission-centered encourages order and stability by integrating fragmented planning pieces into a cohesive whole (Bryson, 1988; Rowley et al., 1997). These plans provide blueprints for future, purposefully directed change precisely because there is a vision toward which the organization moves.

Rowley et al. (1997) insist that in order to be successful in strategic planning, departments, colleges, and universities must revisit the organization's mission and vision statements. They contend that statements such as "we will engage in teaching, research, and service," describe a domain of activity not the direction or purpose of a particular college or university. They suggest that institutions must first think in terms of their actual obligations on campus. To this end, they propose an elaborate ten-step system that begins with identifying key performance indicators (KPIs). KPIs are evidence of what an institution believes it should be doing, which provide the starting point for developing a mission statement that describes a fundamental and unique purpose and the scope of operations and services that it offers (Ireland & Hitt, 1992). A subsequent vision statement must indicate what the institution intends to do, how it identifies its markets, and how it reflects the philosophical premises it uses to guide action.

The development of performance indicators, if they even exist in college and university plans, usually happens during the phase when goals and objectives are set. In practice, most colleges and universities that engage in direction setting activities typically do not go into the details suggested by Rowley et al. They do, however, involve faculty, staff, students, and other stakeholders in crafting a mission and vision statements. In order to fully create a mission statement, the stakeholders must answer the three fundamental questions of "being":

- Who are we?
- What is it that we do, or should do?
- Why do we do it?

The *Who, What,* and *Why* questions get at the core of the institution and thus should lead to a better understanding of its mission. In Chapter 3, we provide two modern day strategic planning success stories, the business schools at the Universities of Maryland and Washington, both of which clearly began strategizing for the future by raising similar questions. It is only after stakeholders create a dialogue around these questions that they are able to discuss questions of action, which eventually get at *How* the institution will realize its mission. Questions of action include:

- Where are we today?
- Where do we want to be in the future? and,
- What do we have to do to get from here to there?

The questions of action help the institution reconcile the ideals of its mission with its current activities and future aspirations and assist it in formulating a vision statement. However, it is the last question, "What do we have to do to get from here to there?" that is really the transition from mission/vision crafting to environmental and organizational analysis, more commonly known as PEST and SWOT analysis.

PEST and SWOT Analysis

Although the particulars of the strategic planning process should be adapted to the uniqueness of the college or university using it, plans for getting from one point to another must consider two key elements: the environment in which the organization exists and its own capacity and resources for change. The broader environment in which higher education operates is defined by Political, Economic, Social, and Technological (PEST) forces. Institutions that profile these forces through a PEST analysis are better able to match their particular Strengths and Weaknesses with Opportunities and Threats (SWOT analysis) that arise from these forces. PEST and SWOT analyses are both critical components of the strategic planning process. When combined and viewed systemically, the four forces in a PEST analysis and the four components of a SWOT analysis create a powerful picture of the inside and outside of an organization.

PEST
The political and economic forces (P and E of PEST) that are part of the context in which higher education operates illustrate how opportunities and threats arise from that context. Political forces at both the federal and state levels, influence higher education institutions. For instance, federal legislation regarding patents and licensing, as we discuss in Chapter 7, has had tremendous impact on the type of research that universities conduct and their motivations for doing so. These laws have presented opportunities for research universities to capture profits from their research discoveries. In contrast, such discoveries in the past were disseminated to the public at large. Similarly, federal reporting requirements and the laws governing where students can use their financial aid have presented opportunities for entire sectors within higher education to go into business (e.g., for-profit proprietary schools).

Public higher education remains primarily a state responsibility, and as such, the values and beliefs of governors and legislators influence the goals and priorities that institutions are able to pursue. Higher education governance structures change through legislative processes, largely because of policymaker attempts to realize political goals, priorities, values, and beliefs. And the results can be mixed depending on the organization and its context. A governance change that centralizes decision making might be viewed as a threat by a university that previously enjoyed great autonomy in defining its direction and purpose, but it might be seen as an opportunity for a small college that previously felt it had no representation in governance at the state-level.

Political forces interact with the economic forces that influence public higher education, largely because political ends often are achieved through budgetary means. To complicate matters further, public funding for higher education is dependent on the global, national, and state economic climates. Public colleges and universities are particularly sensitive to state economic cycles because their funding is partly predicated on state appropriations, which are, in turn, contingent on state tax revenues. Hauptman (1997) has long documented the relationship between economic recession and public funding for higher education. As state tax revenues become strained, higher education appropriations is the first place that policy makers look to cut. Conversely, during economic booms, higher education disproportionately reaps positive benefits (Boyd, 2002; Hovey, 1999). Clearly, funding levels influence institutional opportunities and threats because it is the power of resources that enables institutions to embark on new initiatives or requires that they scale back on existing ones.

Social forces (S in PEST), such as attitudes about the value of education and demographic shifts within the population, constitute a third force, which impacts how colleges and universities function. The value that a social group places on higher education, in part, determines college-going trends among various age groups. If a local economy generates jobs that do not require a college education (e.g., a farm or service economy), and high school graduates can earn an attractive wage by entering the job market directly from high school, they are less likely to attend college than are individuals living within an economy driven by the need for sophisticated technical skills. For instance, the high school-college matriculation rate in Southern Nevada, where the economy is dominated by service-oriented jobs within the gaming industry, hovers around 30%. It is only later in life that individuals in this particular economy look to college as a mechanism for improving their economic and intellectual status.

Demographics in the form of age shifts are more predictable and easier to account for (from an analytical perspective) than are social mores and attitudes. Demographic shifts by age, as a social force, can present opportunities or threats for an institution. Growth in a given population segment (e.g., 18-to 24-year-olds) suggests growth in the demand for higher education services and thus growth in the industry. Stagnant or declining population trends suggest a decline in the demand for higher education services, all else equal.

Institutions that receive public support can underestimate the seriousness of stagnant or declining demand for higher education precisely because they are subsidized. Nonetheless, slow downs driven by demographic shifts are predictable and can be integrated into the planning process. Public universities in North Dakota, for example, have long provided excellent undergraduate education to traditional aged college students. Yet, the 18-to 24-year-old population projections in these states do not paint a promising forecast for industry growth in traditional undergraduate education. Estimates actually suggest a decline in the future (Martinez, 2004). This social force is signaling to public universities in North Dakota that they must increase activity to attract additional 18- to 24-year-olds, recruit out-of-state students, or offer services that are attractive to other age groups.

Technological trends and discoveries, the last force of PEST, dramatically influence higher education on both the teaching and research fronts. Technology enables distance learning in all of its current and emerging forms. New modes of delivery increase the supply of available higher education services, which either intensifies the competition for students or creates new markets. Technology also powers innovation and discovery on the research front. Private industry and government are eager to partner with institutions that create and use technology. Those institutions that discover new technologies or learn how to harness existing ones gain in prestige, power, and additional resources.

SWOT

In higher education, the concept of weakness is much more elusive than the concept of strength, and researchers have found it difficult to use that particular term. Shirley (1988) lumps external threats and internal weaknesses together and calls them constraints (the "what we cannot dos"). Others refer to weaknesses only in terms of resource patterns and program evaluations; as challenges; or as things mandated (what must be done) against resources (what can be done) or institutional needs because weakness implies blame (Doucette, Richardson, & Fenske, 1985; Ziegenfuss, 1989). Throughout the book, we stay with the convention in the strategy literature and use the term weakness to indicate organizational vulnerabilities that currently or potentially hinder the attainment of purpose and goals.

Strengths and weaknesses (SW of SWOT) are best viewed within the context of the opportunities and threats (OT of SWOT) presented by an institution's external environment. An institution's strengths and weaknesses determine whether it can capitalize on an opportunity or constructively navigate a threat. An analysis of strengths and weaknesses relates closely to what has been called analyzing resources and capabilities (Grant, 2005). Universities align resources so that they can realize their goals. Doing so involves taking inventory of what counts as resources, redirecting existing resources, and building and finding new ones. The systematic evaluation of capital provides a set of strategic indicators that colleges and universities can use to assess institutional viability. Taylor and Massey (1996) suggest four distinct types of capital: financial, physical, information, and human. Grant (2005) refers to tangible, intangible, and human resources. Tangible resources include financial and physical resources; intangible resources include technology, reputation, and culture; and human resources include skills and know-how, the capacity for communication and collaboration, and the motivation of the organization to succeed. Although different types of capital can be thought of as distinct in theory, in reality they overlap and relate to each other. For instance, the University of North Carolina is a dominate player in the production of world-class research. The institution's reputation (intangible) continues to fuel its success in obtaining financial and physical resources (tangible), as well as attracting the best human talent (human resources) from around the world.

An opportunity that is ignored or not examined within a particular institution's strengths or weaknesses can quickly become a threat. A major telecommunication firm extended an invitation to State University (we use pseudonyms wherever possible to minimize reputational damage when the examples highlight questionable strategic judgment) to enter into a joint venture. State University officials misinterpreted the costs, ignored the long-term benefits, and decided against the venture. Ultimately, the firm entered into a partnership with another university within the proximate area of State University's campus. Faculty and students at State University lost millions of dollars in research and funding opportunities as a result. State University's miscalculation seems a rarity among institutions, as colleges and universities are more likely to be overambitious and overestimate their capacity.

Institutions that do not have the internal strength to capitalize on external opportunities threaten their own organizational viability. West University (pseudonym) offers a small, but well respected, undergraduate real estate program. Students in the program take specialized courses from one real estate professor, but most of their courses are taught by faculty in other business related fields. Programs in the college are popular and faculty members in the college carry maximum teaching loads. A local real estate developer offered West one million dollars to start a construction management program (a program sometimes offered in tandem with real estate programs). The developer's reputation was not well regarded in the business community, but West saw the opportunity to use the donation to further build its real estate and related programs, along with the commencement of the construction management program. Part of West's excitement for the opportunity to build programs lay in its geographical residence. West is located in a rapidly growing metropolitan area, so it perceived that demand for real estate related programs would grow with the proper resources. West accepted the donation—and its problems began almost immediately. The endowment supported one new construction management faculty position yet enrollments surged in all real estate-related programs except construction management, where enrollments were lower than expected. The real estate program's rapid growth threatened quality. In addition, West's willingness to accept money from the developer led to a drop in donations from other businesses. Because incorrect assumptions drove ill-conceived decisions, what appeared to be an opportunity (a generous donation) coupled with a nonexistent internal strength (adequate faculty numbers and resources) has become a threat to the college's well-being.

Faculty and administrators sometimes know pitifully little about their operations (Keller, 1983, p. 131). It is often the inclusion of outside stakeholders that provide needed perspective, especially in areas of weakness or in the face of impending external threats. PEST and SWOT analyses are enhanced if they are conducted via what is known as a stakeholder assessment. Stakeholder groups exist inside and outside the organization, and their perceptions of the organization and its environment can provide insights otherwise missed if the plan is exclusively constructed by a select few strategists. Asking stakeholders (faculty, staff, students, alumni, policy makers, or community members) what an organization does well, what it can improve, and what unmet opportunities it might address, adds depth to the overall analysis. In addition, this type of assessment helps a university identify pockets of support for initiatives, willing contributors to planned activities, and emerging threats that can derail the best laid plans.

Even though most institutions practice some form of internal assessment, it might not be comprehensive or related to formal planning, especially when consideration of the external environment is ignored. Institution-wide strategic planning efforts many times accept piecemeal self-assessments as substitutes for any rigorous attempt to discover the organization's true strengths and weaknesses. This practice can prove detrimental when the organization receives an unwelcome shock because contextual forces have changed (Peterson, 1980).

The identification of strengths, weaknesses, opportunities, and threats to an institution within a specific political, economic, societal, and technical environment enhances strategy making since the organization gains a "self-awareness" of itself and the landscape on which it operates. At a minimum, PEST and SWOT push institutions to realistically examine their inputs and their capacity to transform those inputs into valuable outputs given the changing and dynamic nature of the environment in which they live. The movement toward progress usually is not immediate, and it is here where goals, objectives and performance measurements provide evidence of movement toward desired ends.

Goals, Objectives, and Performance Measurements

In 1993, the state of Arizona passed legislation mandating that all public agencies, including higher education, complete strategic plans. The state set in place an infrastructure within the Governor's office to monitor and review agency plans to ensure that they were meaningful. The plans were to contain, among other things, goals, objectives, and performance measurements (Franklin, Cawley, & Kachel, 1998). The goals, objectives, and performance measurements were the means toward which the agencies were to work toward achieving their overall missions. The distinction between goals and objectives was one of time. Objectives were akin to short-term goals, to be achieved within a one year period, while goals were three to five years in length. Objectives were also intended to support the goals. A five-year goal of increasing enrollment 10% in programs defined as contributing to economic development might be supported by objectives to increase resources devoted to recruitment efforts targeting those programs. Performance measures were empirically driven and quantitatively and qualitatively defined as inputs, outputs, or outcomes. An input might focus strictly on enrollment, an output on graduation rates, and an outcome on job placement. Higher education institutions, colleges, professional schools (e.g., law schools) and even the board of regents developed strategic plans to comply with the Arizona legislation. Many of the strategic plans developed in the state were exemplary models and helped institutions move toward their purpose.

Goals, objectives, and performance measurements can be crafted at a program, department, college, institution, and even state level. The goals, objectives, and performance measurements must be tied to a purposeful mission and a viable vision of the future, otherwise they exist in a vacuum and are short-lived. The inability to tie measurement to purpose and direction happens at all levels of strategy and planning. For instance, some states have tried to implement "performance funding" for higher education, without attaching the funding to broader policy goals. Performance funding uses performance measurements, which is only one piece of a strategic plan. Unless the measurements fit within a broader framework of policy goals that are aligned with an overarching purpose, it is unlikely such an effort will survive. The state of South Carolina created thirty-eight performance measures (Trombley, 1998), which were not meaningfully tied to a broader purpose or specific policy goals. The effort was eventually abandoned because it was not coherent and the measurements were too diffuse and complex.

WHY STRATEGIC PLANNING FAILS

Even when colleges and universities successfully engage in strategic planning the results can be less than satisfactory. The purpose of planning is coordination, and engaging in strategic planning helps foster organizational stability. It also brings with it the illusion that the organization can master and control its environment. It is a fundamentally conservative process that acts to preserve the basic orientation of the organization (Mintzberg, 1994). In the case of public colleges and universities, where mission is often mandated and vision assumed, such an orientation holds great appeal. In general, though, strategic planning has lost much of its luster and commonly fails for four reasons:

- It's comfortable,
- It precludes an ability on the part of an organization to respond rapidly to changes in the environment,
- It requires commitment but breeds resistance, and
- Once in place it often takes on a life of its own.

Comfort

Strategic planning is comfortable because the end result tends to be generic. Change a few words here and there and the strategic plan for College A becomes the plan for College B. Such a cookie cutter approach to planning in colleges and universities is a logical response given the indistinct nature of most college and university missions. Too many institutions try to be all things to all people, but the predictable result is that their strategic plans lack focus. The final plans are too general, too broad, and reflect a "build it and they will come" mentality of organizations that are guided by euphemistic missions and visions.

Strategic planning is also comfortable because it depends heavily on the past to predict the future. A great deal of time is spent analyzing how to appease as many faculty and administrators as possible. In the end, what action occurs tends to be incremental at best—safe, incremental change. Finally, and perhaps most pernicious, strategic planning is comfortable because it is a process that is well defined and familiar to most administrators with significant experience. Strategic planning, therefore, easily serves as a symbol that something is being done and efforts are being made to make changes.

Response Time

Strategic planning in higher education institutions is often an exercise in consensus building at the rank and file levels, which adds to the incremental approach to change inherent in the process. Incremental change hinders an institution's ability to respond to unanticipated occurrences in the environment. An obsession with control and the illusion that we have it encourages conformity, and it down plays the role of intuition (Mintzberg, 1994). Such inflexibility stifles creativity and discourages initiative and any attempt at innovative behavior. In the extreme, institutions engage in only those activities mandated by the strategic plan. In a large planning exercise where college-level priorities, given an overarching university plan, are accumulated and fed upward through the system, little or no opportunity exists for injecting fresh insights about the future. The planning mechanism overwhelms the thought process and the plan becomes an unrealistic wish list. In such instances, plans are used to justify wants rather than to anticipate needs, and ultimately they lessen the chance of identifying and responding to truly exploitable opportunities.

Resistance Instead of Commitment

Strategic plans reflect an attempt to objectively limit choice. Attempts at objectivity effectively reduce overall commitment to the plan, especially at the time of implementation. Commitment to action grows out of personal control and a sense of ownership, and although strategic planning appears on the surface to be inclusive, decisions at the top, not suggestions from the ranks, typically dictate priorities. As a consequence, the top down tendency of strategic planning at colleges and universities breeds resistance instead of commitment. Strategic planning becomes a game where insiders (faculty and staff) don't believe in it but influential leaders (administrators, boards of regents, and state legislators) do. In some instances, it becomes a well-publicized, politically necessary process, decorative but not particularly functional. Faculty members who perceive that the planning process is merely symbolic or that they have a minor role in working on substantive elements of the plan are likely to resist subsequent efforts that support the plan.

A Life of Its Own

Strategic planning's final flaw stems from its propensity toward self- sustainability. Once in place, even when revisited, a strategic plan is rarely comprehensively evaluated (Mintzberg, 1994). Pfeffer and Sutton (2006) state that because strategic planning is often linked to budgeting, it is a process that consumes enormous time and resources, which once invested are hard for an institution to abandon. Hope and Fraser (2003) found that the average time consumed by strategic planning can take between four and five months and consume 20 to 30% of managerial time. The premium placed on decision making by consensus in higher education has additional implications for the time and resource commitments inherent in strategic planning. In colleges and universities, strategic planning committees typically consist of faculty, staff, and administrators. It is plausible that even if faculty and staff are debating broad-based strategies, the time involved is greater than is true in for-profit organizations precisely because of the tradition of consensus. The hard work and time investment in the strategic planning process then become ends in themselves. If goals, objectives, or key performance indicators come into question, the tendency is to defend and preserve what exists because it was the result of great time and effort, and few people have the energy to repeat the process all over again. In short, the existing strategic plan takes on a life of its own.

CONCLUSION

For many institutions, strategic planning is a firmly entrenched process. Different components of strategic plans often appear in individual documents, standalone initiatives, or as singular pieces that inform the strategy-making process. Indeed, strategic planning provides many valuable tools, but it does have its drawbacks. In Chapter 3, we offer higher education related examples of when strategic planning works and when it fails. At the end of Chapter 3 we suggest application questions and templates for each of the strategic planning components.

CHAPTER 3

STRATEGIC PLANNING

Lessons and Applications

Today, strategic planning is a firmly entrenched process in higher education. In some states, it is not only encouraged but mandated. For instance, the New Jersey Institute of Technology Act of 1995 specifies that the New Jersey Institute of Technology (NJIT) must develop an institutional plan and determine the schools, departments, programs, and degree levels to be offered by the institution consistent with that plan.

For many within college and universities, strategic planning has become a required task that is imposed on resistant faculty who do not trust each other, let alone the university administrators and state legislators who insist on their engagement in the process. In the end, the strategic planning process might produce voluminous documents which, at best, provide some semblance of institutional thinking about purpose and direction. At worst, the documents represent an exercise in collecting murky data to support the conflicting wish lists of administrators and faculty. In such situations, the enterprise's greatest strength—faculty autonomy and individuality—becomes its weakest link. Instead of pulling together, faculty pull apart, protecting turf and defending a way of life that in some instances is rapidly slipping away. It doesn't have to be.

Innovative Strategy Making in Higher Education, pages 25–44
Copyright © 2009 by Information Age Publishing
All rights of reproduction in any form reserved.

STRATEGIC PLANNING WHEN IT WORKS

Within the past ten years, the business schools at the Universities of Maryland (UM) and Washington (UW) have strategically positioned themselves as premiere, innovative MBA programs that are consistently ranked within the top fifty in the nation (Wolverton & Penley, 2004). Each school moved within a relatively short time from being thought of as sound, with perhaps a bright spot here or there, to colleges with international stature. In each instance, strategic planning, or at least elements of it, helped sharpen purpose and intent and directly contributed to the elevated status of the schools.

In the late 1990s and early 2000s, the Maryland (Frank, 2004) and Washington (Gupta, 2004) business schools suffered from the same malady: they wanted to do and be good at everything. The end result: both schools provided programs indistinguishable from other moderately good programs. Funding and community support languished. Faculty worked within insular fiefdoms protecting territorial rights. In both cases, however, the strategic planning process provided a vehicle by which administrators and faculty could work together toward a common end. This collective endeavor also created a college culture that encouraged teamwork and collaboration. It is not that each of these schools followed a rigidly defined strategic planning process, but they did use major tenets and ideas of strategic planning to move in a desired direction. Within ten years, both schools were highly rated among their national peers, and there is no doubt that strategic planning played a role in getting them there.

The University of Maryland Business School

Maryland's dean was hired, at least in part, because he could articulate a vision for the college: to be the leading technology-oriented business school in the nation. With the direction set, he engaged the faculty in the school's first strategic planning exercise. He began by asking them two questions: What does it mean to be a leading technologically oriented business school? And, what should such an orientation mean in terms of rankings, environment, and students? Answers to these questions generated three specific targets:

- To become one of the top fifteen business schools in the U.S.,
- To provide a supportive research and teaching environment for faculty and students, and
- To give graduates a first-class return on investment for their time and expenses.

The three targets set by faculty encompass two very important components of strategic planning: goals and measurements. The first target is both a goal and a measurement. The goal of reaching top-fifteen status is quantitatively measurable, as yearly publications rank business schools. The second and third targets are, admittedly, harder to measure, but laudable goals just the same.

Faculty then embarked on an assessment process by examining the school's strengths and weaknesses, which is a central theme of SWOT analysis. The school's strengths included a fairly strong MBA program, several excellent PhD specializations, outstanding faculty research productivity, and potential cross-functional program efforts already in progress. They also identified weaknesses. Business school faculty taught 10% of the university's total credit hours but represented less than 5% of the university's total faculty. No specialty programs ranked in the top twenty-five nationally. Recognition by other business school deans, MBA directors, and corporate recruiters was low. Job placement of graduates was sub par. The school lacked sufficient support for PhD students; faculty salaries were not competitive; their physical plant was too small; and they engaged in little alumni development.

From an industry standpoint, Maryland (UM) competed for students with a number of very good business schools in Washington, DC. These schools exploited governmental connections, whereas UM had not capitalized on its close proximity to political and international resources located less than twenty miles away. The UM business school had no idea how to distinguish its programs. To complicate matters further, UM is not located in an industrial center, so it had entered into few corporate partnerships. Because Maryland residents did not think of it as their school, the school also lacked local and regional support. Finally, the university viewed the business school as a cash cow and had no problem "milking" it while providing limited fiscal support.

Guided by its three targets and based on a thorough strengths and weaknesses analysis, the school set six priorities that related to the targets. UM also identified specific activities to move toward those priorities, along with the parties responsible for implementing the activities. The school restructured departments, built new technology-based programs, developed marketing strategies, worked to redistribute faculty teaching loads and hired new faculty, expanded school facilities, and began the process of engaging the local community and school alumni. UM's many actions were nicely coordinated because the targets and reinforcing priorities guided the process. Moving up in the national rankings provided evidence that the school's planning efforts had worked.

The University of Washington Business School (UW)

UW faculty began with a vague notion that something needed to be done. They hired a new dean known for driving change. He came into the position with no preconceived notions about where the school should head but with a commitment to transform the school and a keen idea of how to proceed. He asked all faculty to finish the statement: I would be proud of this school if....

The dean hired expert facilitators and assembled a strategy team. Unlike Maryland, where faculty represented the key strategists, Washington involved representatives from faculty, staff, students, alumni, advisory boards (external community), and UW central administration. This group identified paradoxes, which were very much equated with weaknesses within the school:

- The business school was located in one of the nation's hotbeds of entrepreneurship, but it provided conventional, non-innovative programming.
- Risk taking is a key component of entrepreneurship, but the school was risk averse.
- More than 20,000 of its 35,000 alumni lived within the Seattle metropolitan area and many of them held key leadership positions in some of the largest companies in the country, yet the school remained isolated.
- Key technology-related industries are based in Seattle, yet the school's programs were broad based and unfocused.

From this process, a very clear vision statement emerged: *We are an entrepreneurial learning community dedicated to the creation, application, and sharing of knowledge that places special emphasis on high-technology business environments.* (Although stated in the present tense, this statement clearly points to where the school wanted to go, not to where it was at that specific point in time). A list of five goals followed: improve student learning; promote a collegial, supportive environment; implement fair and equitable personnel policies; provide the necessary technological support for faculty, students, and staff; and achieve sufficient resource to compete with peer institutions.

The school developed several new technology management programs and a technology center. It reframed how it looked at alumni and business community members. The need for new resources was critical, and the school asked for time, expertise, and advice from a wide array of stakeholders. In return, the school asked what it could do to help alumni and local businesses meet their goals. Mutuality builds trust and the foundation for strong alliances. UW's open and honest approach resulted in not only increased private donations but increased state legislative support as well.

Externally, the school measured advisory board members' involvement and produced a corporate score card, which grades corporations on involvement in terms of mentorships, internships, classroom involvement, research projects, advisory board involvement, and hiring practices (i.e., are they hiring our graduates). Internally, the school put several questions at the forefront of its efforts and sought to continually ask itself if it was accomplishing the inherent goals embedded in the questions:

- Are we transforming the students' learning experience?
- Have we implemented personnel polices that will reward those people who are advancing the mission of the school?
- Are faculty engaged with industry?
- What investments in technology infrastructure are we making that allow our students and faculty to implement our mission?
- How are we moving to attract resources to keep up with our peers?

These two report cards, corporate and school, which are shared widely with UW's constituency base, signal the dedication that the business school has to getting it right and encourages further targeted participation on the part of all parties.

UW's process started with an assessment of facts that pointed to several weaknesses. The school's vision statement emerged from this process, as did meaningful goals and questions. The report cards were excellent performance measures to help the school assess its progress along the way. External and internal stakeholders maintained interest and involvement to move the organization toward its goals. UW, like Maryland, demonstrates that strategic planning is often a customized process not amenable to formulaic methods. Instead, its value lies in helping organizations forge toward a successful future.

STRATEGIC PLANNING WHEN IT FAILS

Although the many shortcomings of strategic planning have been well documented (Mintzberg, 1994; Pfeffer & Sutton, 2006), perhaps the issues of comfort and resistance are the two most prominent reasons the process often fails within the higher education environment. The process becomes comfortable because the strategies are generic enough that nobody need disagree on them. In addition, it is easy to interpolate the future because we simply rely on what has happened in the past, and most administrators know how to form committees and take other steps to complete the motions involved in the strategic planning process. Weisbord (1996) states that managers often fall back on the familiar, traveling through the old processes, structures, and systems even though the problems and challenges are new. New managers, for example, will implement processes they have used in the past in new environments, or change organizational structures to reflect those that worked in previous settings. Similarly, chairs, deans, provosts, and presidents know the strategic planning process, and it is this familiarity that breeds comfort and discourages them from using new tools and strategies that might be useful in moving toward the future. The generic outcomes associated with strategic planning, coupled with the large time investment of committee work, breeds negativity and resistance. These sentiments are directed toward those involved in creating the plan, and those charged with carrying out the work, especially if the work on one strategic plan commences because the previous one has been nullified by a change in leadership.

Southern Community College

Southern Community College (pseudonym) went through its first real strategic planning process in the mid-1990s. Southern started out as a 2,000 student campus in the early 1970s, but headcount enrollment grew to more than 13,000 by 1990. Its only president had presided over an extended period of growth and prosperity. The climate had changed at the start of the new decade, though, and the president felt the increasing strain of unpredictable state appropriations to the college because of the recession in the early 1990s. At the same time, an anti-tax sentiment across the state meant that local funding sources were no longer automatic. The community had historically passed bond initiatives to build additional facilities at the college, but the latest initiative was voted down by a slim margin.

Grumblings between faculty and staff soon began to surface as resource constraints became a reality. Students, parents, and local businesses also voiced concerns about Southern's ability to meet community needs. The president felt trapped from all sides and implemented a strategic planning process, a common solution touted among his peers from across the nation. The president had enjoyed hero-like status over his twenty-year tenure, so his charismatic pronouncement of the strategic planning process and the promise of its outcomes to get the college back on track were met with much enthusiasm. The president organized four college-level committees: curriculum and programs, facilities and technology, faculty and staff, and students. The college level committees comprised faculty, staff, and students from across the college. The committees were charged with assessing the internal state of affairs in their given areas vis-à-vis the environment. Each committee was then to draft goals, objectives, and measures in its given area. In addition to the four college-level committees, each department within the college was to establish its direction guided by its mission and supported by its goals and objectives. The president emphasized that the department work was critical because it would (a) reinforce the work of the college-level committees, and (b) could be used for accreditation purposes. Every committee was to follow the lead of a special presidential committee, which was charged with updating and drafting mission and vision statements for the college. All strategic plans, at all levels, were to reinforce the overall mission.

The total strategic planning effort was three months into the new academic year when the president unexpectedly announced his retirement due to an illness, starting in the spring semester. An interim president was hired for the spring semester, and a national search for a new president was on. The interim president had no interest in the full-time presidency, so he "froze" the strategic planning process, suspecting that a new president would quite possibly want to set a new and different direction.

The eventual incoming president informed the board of regents and the search committee that he was committed to the spirit and intent of strategic planning. Upon his hiring in the summer, the new president did announce his plans to reignite the strategic planning process at the start of the fall semester. The president's direction and priorities were a bit different, however, so he redefined the four previous college-level committees into three: community and workforce development, curriculum, and students. The president believed that faculty issues would surface in the other committees, and issues of technology would naturally accompany discussions across all the committees.

This new strategic planning effort took a total of six months and ran into the middle of the spring semester. All documents were finalized and all committee work was pronounced complete. The spring semester ended with a memo from the president saying that some new workforce development programs would be started in the fall to take advantage of the results of the strategic planning process. Several administrators and faculty complained among themselves that the workforce development programs were not as much a reflection of the strategic plan as they were a mirror of the president's prior experience at another institution—he was doing what he knew, just at a new institution.

The new semester started, and several new workforce development programs were initiated at the president's behest. Aside from the new programs, there was little evidence that any other activity within the college was driven by the strategic plan. In fact, even at the department levels, there were few attempts at data collection since upper administration did not follow through on requests for updates on goals or measurements. Most people felt the strategic planning process was an exhaustive process that led nowhere. Within a year, the president was fired by the board of regents for a series of missteps. Faculty and staff yearned for the growth and continuity of the early years, but they knew they would soon be in the throes of hiring a third president in as many years. Each of the three finalists for the new search was asked about strategic planning during the on campus interview. Each finalist professed a belief in the efficacy and necessity of strategic planning at any community college. By this time, faculty and staff at Southern had an aversion and resistance to any more strategic planning initiatives, yet strategic planning had apparently become a mainstay between community colleges and their leaders.

OPERATIONALIZING STRATEGIC PLANNING

Chapter 2 contains a discussion of mission, PEST, SWOT, goals, and performance measures. Examples accompany much of the narrative in chapter 2, so, for instance, the discussion on performance measures becomes tangible rather than abstract and theoretical. In the final sections of this chapter, we briefly review strategic planning in general and how it relates to higher education. This overview is followed by reviews of each major strategic planning component, along with a number of questions to help guide the strategic planning process.

The Strategic Planning Process

One of the longstanding criticisms of strategic planning in the business world is that it is a mechanical process that must be performed in a sequence of linear steps. Organizations are first encouraged to define a mission and set a vision, produce PEST and SWOT analyses, create goals, and generate corresponding performance measures. Finally, there is an evaluation process that must assess the effectiveness of the program. Although the sequence of the steps is theoretically sound, the reality is that effective strategic planning is a nonlinear process whereby steps can overlap or occur out of sequence. Some steps might require revision, given new information or additional insights by strategists. The development of goals and vision might happen concurrently; or ambitions to realize certain performance might in fact drive the derivation of the goals and the vision or mission. Some organizations critically analyze the economic and technological possibilities within their environment but give little attention to political or social factors, while other organizations focus on strengths and weaknesses but do not explicitly document opportunities and threats.

Certainly, there are similarities among higher education institutions that effectively use strategic planning (or elements of it) as a strategy tool. Colleges and universities that successfully engage in strategic planning craft the process to fit their particular cultures, and they use strategic planning as a way to build on their strengths and eradicate their weaknesses. In higher education, as in business, we have examples of how organizational leaders use strategic planning in a variety of ways. For instance, a college dean might start with a specific direction in mind as in the case of the business school at Maryland. Or he or she might begin at a more fundamental level by saying "we need to redefine who we are by identifying some paradoxes that point out our weaknesses," as was the case at Washington's business school.

Participation can vary. At Maryland's business school, no clear external community support existed, and few alumni were involved with the school's strategic planning process. As a consequence, organizational and environmental analyses were internally executed; and, together, the dean and faculty determined how the school would realize its mission and vision. In contrast, stakeholders at the business school at the University of Washington sensed a need for change, recognized that the local economy should drive, at least in part, the direction in which the school should move, and identified influential alumni that could help the school. UW's dean involved multiple internal and external stakeholder groups in setting both the direction and how to get from where the school was to where it wanted (needed) to be. In both examples, stakeholders sought ways to create organizational distinctiveness by taking into account unique contextual circumstances. The primary object: enhanced organizational success. The driving impetus: fiscal well-being.

No two organizations approach strategic planning in exactly the same way. All, however, seem to define goals and measures to some degree; they identify at least some organizational characteristics to compare against the environmental context; and they develop the major actions that are needed to accomplish their defined organizational goals. The monitoring and evaluation of progress may occur through the formal creation of key performance indicators or externally generated rankings over which the institution has little control. Whatever the case, informed choices get made that allow colleges and universities to negotiate uncertain waters and move toward a defined purpose.

Keller (1983) is largely credited with being the first to provide tools to the higher education industry to help institutions operationalize the strategic planning process. Keller's (1983) strategic analysis framework focuses on SWOT and is simply divided into an internal and external appraisal. The simplicity of the framework correlates to its usability. The internal analysis consists of appraising institutional history, traditions, values, and aspirations for the future; academic strengths and weaknesses; financial strengths and weaknesses; and priorities of leadership.

Keller's external analysis demonstrates that the classic components of strategic planning are not so neatly divided, and there is often a crossover between these components. An analysis of opportunities and threats (OT of SWOT) can naturally generate questions or issues related to a PEST analysis. For example, Keller's external analysis encourages leaders to examine demographic shifts (S in PEST), market preferences, and the actions of their competitors.

Most college and university administrators have at one time or another engaged in strategic planning exercises. Those who do choose to use strategic planning should best think of it as a contribution to strategy making but at the same time realize that the strategic plan alone does not constitute a comprehensive organizational strategy. Tools, such as Keller's, are useful in guiding the process since strategic planning necessitates some level of coordination given that multiple people and committees are involved over a sustained period of time. In the spirit of helping leaders further organize the strategic planning process, the five guides below capture the major components commonly equated with strategic planning: mission and vision, PEST, SWOT, goals and objectives, and performance measures. We also add a sixth component called action plans, which aide in the actual implementation of strategy.

The questions and issues within the guides lend structure to the strategic planning process, but they in no way suggest an absolute step-by-step sequence. Different organizations will approach strategic planning differently and thus emphasize its components differently. Some planners might use the guides in sequence. Others will borrow only certain questions and make them the focus of the strategic planning effort.

Guide for Mission and Vision Statement Formation

The terms mission, mission statement, and vision statement are often used interchangeably, but they are distinct. The mission of a public institution reflects its legislated purpose and the core values that underscore its existence. It is usually broad, comprehensive, somewhat ambiguous, and rarely changed. For public colleges and universities, missions and their accompanying statements change when a legislative body authorizes the change. For example, Tempe Normal School became Arizona State College, which became Arizona State University only after legislative action in the first case and a statewide voter referendum forced the legislature to make the change in the second. In each instance, the institution's mission fundamentally shifted from preparing teachers in two years to providing four-year undergraduate education to conducting research.

Because the mission speaks to the organization's purpose, it should address the question of "what are we charged to do?" New Mexico State University's mission makes it clear what the state legislature has charged it to do. Its mission states (www.nmsu.edu, retrieved, January 31, 2008):

> The mission of New Mexico State University is to serve the people of New Mexico through education, research, extension education, and public service, with special emphasis on preserving the state's multi-cultural heritage, protecting its environment, and fostering its economic development in an interdependent world. New Mexico State University is an equal opportunity institution welcoming all within our community, regardless of age, ancestry, color, disability, gender, national origin, race, religion, sexual orientation, or veteran status.
>
> **Education**
>
> The first responsibility of the university is to provide quality education. As the state's land-grant institution, New Mexico State is committed to serving the educational needs of a student body of various ages, interests, and cultural backgrounds. The university seeks to educate each student not only in how to earn a living but also in how to live a meaningful life.
>
> **Research**
>
> Advancing knowledge and enriching culture are the goals of education, so they are primary objectives of the university. From its beginnings as a land-grant university, New Mexico State has endorsed the concept that strong programs of research and other creative endeavors provide the basis for strong academic programs. Faculty, professional staff, and students engage in creative activities and conduct and propagate the results of basic and applied research in virtually every discipline, often under external sponsorship and with the assistance of numerous specialized campus institutes, centers, and laboratories.
>
> **Extension Education**
>
> A unique responsibility of a land-grant university is providing informal, off-campus educational programs through the Cooperative Extension Service. New Mexico State University, in partnership with federal, state, and county governments, is committed to extending research-based knowledge throughout the state.
>
> **Public Service**
>
> A major tradition of land-grant colleges is dedication to public service. New Mexico State University is committed to providing specialized assistance, information, and programs designed to meet educational, cultural, and economic needs of the state.

In contrast to an organization's mission, its mission statement, which can also be somewhat ambiguous, usually gets at what an organization currently does. It is an abbreviated statement that captures the essence of the mission. New Mexico State's mission statement, which flows from its mission states:

> New Mexico State University is the state's land grant university, serving the educational needs of New Mexico's diverse population through comprehensive programs of education, research, extension education, and public service.

People often confuse mission with vision. A mission is not action-oriented but a vision is. Vision statements indicate the way in which the institution intends to fulfill its mission—the direction it plans to take. They are future oriented. Vision statements should be short and concise, fluid, and can change over time, quite often with a change in leadership.

New Mexico State's vision statement sets a direction and stretches the institution.

> By 2020, New Mexico State University (NMSU) will be a premier university as evidenced by demonstrated and quantifiable excellence in teaching, research, and service relative to its peer institutions.

Strategists often develop the mission and vision in conjunction, or create a hybrid statement of sorts. The University of Washington's business school statement (*we are an entrepreneurial learning community dedicated to the creation, application, and sharing of knowledge that places special emphasis on high-technology business environment*) can be considered a hybrid in that it is stated as fact but clearly points to where the school wants to be, not where it was when the statement was written. Whatever strategy an organization takes, the following questions can serve as guides to help the institution test the viability of a mission and/or vision.

Questions to Test the Viability of Mission and Vision Statements
- What is our underlying charge?
- Does our mission reflect that charge?
- Does the mission statement clearly state what our business is, or "What we do as an organization?"
- Does it reflect the essence of our mission?
- Does our mission statement speak to "Why we do what we do?" (Importance)
- Does our vision statement speak to where we want to be in the future?
- Does our vision statement reinforce our mission?
- Does the vision statement broadly identify the outcomes we are after?

- Does it reflect what we value?
- Can the average employee read the mission and vision statements and make sense of them?
- Can an external stakeholder read the mission and vision statements and make sense of them?

Guide for PEST

The PEST analysis focuses specifically on external, or environmental, factors that influence the effectiveness of the organization. Many strategic planners do not dedicate a substantial amount of time to a PEST analysis because it is a macro exercise that simply draws attention to broad boundaries that organizational leaders cannot control. Although it is true that most factors within a PEST analysis are not controlled by any one organization, it is important to highlight those factors because they can point to promising or perilous options for organizational action. On the balance, it is probably sound advice to not spend an inordinate amount of time on a PEST analysis, but it is also a mistake to ignore it.

The following questions can serve as a guide to help monitor the macro components of the environment. The political questions are broken down into federal and state components. Higher education is largely a state function, but federal policies related to student aid, accountability, and research play a potential role in institutional strategy.

Questions to Guide the PEST Analysis

Political

- Federal: Are there any changes in student financial aid that will help or hinder student access to our institution? If so, what are they? And, how will they impact access?
- Federal: Are there changes in accountability policy that will influence the reporting requirements for our institution? If so, what are they? And, what will the impact be?
- Federal: Do recent research funding opportunities exist that are aligned with our institution's mission or vision? If so, what are they? And, how can we take advantage of them?
- State: Are key political leaders in our state generally engaged and interested in higher education issues? In what ways? How can we take advantage of this interest? If not, how can we build interest?
- State: Are key political leaders in our state interested in initiating state-level governance changes in higher education? What specifically? What is the potential impact?

- State: How do political leaders view universities? Community colleges? Private institutions and for-profit providers? How might their attitudes affect us?
- State: What key changes in state law could impact this institution? In what ways?

Economic
- Is the state economy growing or experiencing a downturn? To what degree?
- What is the likely picture for state revenues, in the immediate future?
- Is our state highly dependent on sales taxes (as opposed to personal income taxes)? If yes, higher education appropriations are more susceptible to swings in the economy and forecasts should account for this reality.
- What efforts to attract new revenue-generating industries into the state are being pursued? How might any such efforts impact this institution?

Social
- What is the five-year forecast for changes in 5–17 year-olds?
- What is the five-year forecast for changes in 18–24 year-olds?
- What is the five-year forecast for changes in 25–49 year-olds?
- What other demographic changes (perhaps ones that are more difficult to quantify) are likely to impact enrollment in the next five years? For instance, in- or out-migration.
- What is the attitude of state residents about the importance or relevance of a college education?

Technological
- What is our state's technological capability, in terms of tracking students and/or tracking institutional performance?
- What technologies exist that might be integrated into the operation of our institution?
- What technologies are on the horizon that might change or alter the operation/academic offerings and/or research endeavors of our institution?

Guide for SWOT

Keller's framework provides a fine starting point for creating a SWOT analysis because he speaks to internal capabilities, such as history and organizational capacity, and external factors that can reveal opportunities and threats. Our guide is a complement to Keller's work and meant to build on it. Although Keller implicitly integrates elements of PEST into his framework, we directly mesh all the elements of PEST into the opportunities and threats portion of SWOT.

Guides for the Strengths and Weaknesses (SW of SWOT) Analysis

An analysis of the strengths and weaknesses of an institution should provide the information with which to answer the questions: who are we and where are we now? The three categories below create a descriptive profile of the institution.

Overview of Institutional Scope and Function
- Statutory basis of institution (if any)
- Historical perspective: Date created
- Historical perspective: Significant events that have shaped or influenced the institution
- Major institutional accomplishments
- Public perception
- Public expectations

Institutional Factors
- Size and composition of workforce (number, gender, racial composition, professional, clerical, classified, professorial ranks, areas of faculty expertise, etc.)
- Current organizational structure (number of colleges, departments, centers/institutes, support functions, etc.)
- Current or past leaders or organizational changes that carry lasting influence for the organization today (e.g., reorganizations, responsibility-based budgeting)
- Geographic location advantages and disadvantages
- Information resource management capability
- Capital improvement needs
- Human resource status: turnover, morale, experience levels (e.g., full professors versus assistants), training infrastructure
- Programs and pockets of excellence (instructional, research, service, administrative)
- Missing programs (instructional, research, service, administrative)

Fiscal Operations
- Size of budget
- Nature of cost structure (or even defining one's cost structure)
- Composition of revenue sources (and trends)

- Efficiency of internal accounting and finance procedures
- Flexibility of funding (can current resources be redirected?)

Guide for the Opportunities and Threats (OT of SWOT) Analysis

The examination of opportunities and threats should be conducted in two stages. The first stage should take into consideration the PEST analysis of the external environment. This examination answers the question: do we know our context?

Political
- Examine the Political questions in the PEST analysis. Do the answers to any of these questions reveal potential opportunities or threats for our institution?

Economic
- Examine the Economic questions in the PEST analysis. Do the answers to any of these questions reveal potential opportunities or threats for our institution? Do the answers to these questions suggest challenges to our existing cost or revenue structure, or perhaps a need to try to shift the composition of those structures? Can we find new resources?

Social
- Examine the Social questions in the PEST analysis. Do the answers to these questions reveal potential opportunities or threats for our institution? Do the answers to these questions suggest a need to create new services or revise existing ones to meet changing demographic needs based on trends?

Technological
- Examine the Technological questions in the PEST analysis. Do the answers to these questions reveal potential opportunities or threats for our institution?

The second stage of the examination requires that institutions examine their strengths and weaknesses in terms of the perceived external opportunities and threats. Each of these factors suggests a strength or weakness. Once a strength/weakness profile is created, three questions about strengths and weaknesses remain:

- In what ways could this strength become a weakness?
- In what ways could this weakness become a strength?
- What would it take to turn a weakness into a strength?

The notion is to identify strengths that will clearly allow the institution to take advantage of current or emerging opportunities while minimizing weaknesses that allow threats to seep into the organization. Threats are averted by (a) revealing situations in which the organization should forego a perceived opportunity because of a lack of resources and (b) identifying areas that need to be strengthened because to leave them unattended will threaten institutional viability. All PEST and SWOT analysis leads to the same goal: to reveal an understanding of the institution and the context in which it operates, where it needs to go, and what resources it needs to get there.

Guide for Goals and Objectives

The creation of either a mission or vision statement is a high-level exercise that speaks generally to the organization. PEST and SWOT analyses, although revealing specific factors that can influence the success of an institution, remain necessarily broad. As noted in Chapter 2, mission statements, PEST, and SWOT speak to the *Who, What* and *Why* of the organization. The development of goals begins to lay the groundwork for more specifically indicating *How* the organization will realize its mission while moving toward its vision for the future, given what currently exists.

A goal is a desired end result, and every goal should be embodied in a clear and succinct statement. Objectives are sub-goals that support an overarching goal and provide a more concrete target that is clearly measurable. New Mexico State's plan has five goals, each with four to six objectives. Goal One and its two accompanying objectives provide a good example:

> *Goal 1*: To be nationally and internationally recognized for its academic programs at all levels (two-year, undergraduate, and graduate).

> *Objective 1*: Attract increasing numbers of well-qualified students at all academic levels
> *Objective 2*: Enroll a competitive proportion of students from New Mexico two-year institutions.

Goals typically range from two to five years, or longer in NMSU's case (it sees completion of its goals and the realization of its vision by 2020 as a far reaching plan). Objectives tend to be more immediate and are usually one year in scope. An institution can simplify its planning process by creating goals but not objectives. In this case, the targeted completion of a goal might range from one to five years. The time frame for a goal can extend beyond this range as in New Mexico's case, but in a dynamic, changing environment, long-term goals require review every third year—even if it is certain that they will extend into the future. Waiting five or more years to confirm or revise goals is risky in an uncertain environment.

For purposes of illustration, we provide a guide for creating sound goals, but a similar guide could easily be developed for objectives.

Questions to Test the Viability of Goal Statements
- Does the goal support the mission?
- Is the goal consistent with our statutory existence or legislative authority?
- Does the goal help us realize our vision?
- Does the goal deal with just one issue (it should not be multidimensional)?
- Does the goal require a result that can be reasonably measured?
- Can the goal be associated with an activity that can contribute to its accomplishment?
- Is the goal sufficiently challenging that it will stretch the organization but not too unrealistic that it will assure failure?
- Is the goal meaningful to internal stakeholders?
- Is the goal meaningful to external stakeholders?

Guide for Performance Measures

Performance measures are the "meat and potatoes" of implementing a plan because they are the indicators of progress that provide necessary feedback to management, employees, and stakeholders. The task is to search for indicators that can reasonably be measured, either qualitatively or quantitatively, so that there is some systematic sense of whether the organization is accomplishing its mission and moving toward its vision through the accomplishment of its goals. Every goal or objective should have at least one associated performance measure.

> *Goal:* To serve as an engine for economic, social, educational, and community development.

> *Objective:* Encourage university–community collaborations.

> *Measure for Objective:* Increase the number of university–community collaborations across all colleges.

Multiple objectives and accompanying performance measures for the same goal should be somewhat correlated but also examine and measure the goal from slightly different perspectives. On a cautionary note: goals with too many performance measures make the goal almost impossible to achieve because the measurements often produce contradictory and conflicting results.

Questions to Test the Viability of Performance Measures
- Does the performance measure relate to the mission of the organization?
- Does the performance measure relate to the vision of the organization?
- Does the performance measure relate to the goal it represents?
- Is it possible to collect accurate and reliable quantitative data for this performance measurement?
- Is it possible to collect qualitative data, by observation, interviews, or any other means, for this performance measurement?
- Does the performance measurement relate to other measurements for the same goal but not duplicate them?

Guide for Action Plans

Action plans are work plans. They identify tasks, assign responsibility, and provide a timetable. An action plan is comprised of action statements. In today's environment, the majority of workers are most satisfied when they know what end goal they are working toward without having the means painstakingly defined for them. Action plans (and their associated statements) must provide some detail but leave flexibility for employees to deal with unanticipated challenges. Action statements usually begin with action words. In fact, effective action plans are broken down into steps. The steps are simple and commonly articulated in one concise sentence. The following example illustrates a goal and associated action statements for the financial aid office at an institution.

Goal: To provide institutional aid to students in a more timely manner.

Action 1: Identify possible office processes that can slow timeliness
(Deadline: March 15, 2008; Responsibility: office supervisor).
Action 2: Identify possible student actions that can slow timeliness
(Deadline: April 15, 2008; Responsibility: senior analyst).

Action 3: Review existing reports for duplications or contradictory
student information (Deadline: May 15, 2008; Responsibility:
Assistant Director of Financial Aid).

Action 4: Develop a list of solutions to improve timeliness, including resource needs (Deadline: June 15, 2008; Responsibility: Director
of Financial Aid).

The following questions can serve as a guide to test the viability of action
statements.

Questions to Test the Viability of Action Statements
- Does the action statement relate to the goal?
- Does the action statement contain a call to perform some sort of
  activity?
- Does the action statement contain a time frame for completion?
- Does the action statement assign responsibility for action to a group
  or individual?
- Are reasonable resources (staff, time, technology) available to com-
  plete the action step?

CLOSING COMMENTS

A contributing factor to the abandonment of strategic planning in the business arena is that leaders became disenchanted with the time and resources
that it took to complete the entire process. Strategic planning also became
a mechanical, linear process, more equated with inflexibility than innovation and creativity. True strategic planning requires thinking, flexibility,
and leadership discretion. If leaders have properly used strategic planning
as a strategy tool, they will be able to answer several questions after implementation has taken root: Have we done what we set out to do? Where have
we failed? Why? Where should we direct (or redirect) our efforts?

CHAPTER 4

ANALYZING HIGHER EDUCATION AS AN INDUSTRY

Peterson and Dill (1997) define three eras that characterize the evolution of the higher education industry: Traditional Higher Education, Mass Higher Education, and Postsecondary Education. Prior to 1950, the higher education industry was primarily associated with four-year institutions, or traditional higher education. The momentum for mass higher education began in the 1950s, largely on the heels of the Truman Commission Report in 1948, which recommended higher education for everyone who graduates from high school. The community college movement followed, and with it an increasingly diverse array of students. The 1970s solidified the postsecondary education era with the infusion of federal aid. Students were free to use federal aid at two- and four-year colleges and universities and proprietary institutions as well.

A new era has emerged in the higher education industry, which we term the Global Postsecondary Education and Training era. Table 2 shows the progression of the eras as defined by Peterson and Dill and adds the new era to reflect 2000 and beyond.

The Global Postsecondary Education and Training industry includes new organizational entities that compete with higher education institutions associated with the postsecondary industry. It is a strategic error for col-

Innovative Strategy Making in Higher Education, pages 45–61
45

TABLE 2   The Evolving Higher Education Industry

Era	Approximate Timeframe	Structural Characteristics	Major Associated Events
Traditional Higher Education	1940s–1960s	Public and Private Four-Year Institutions, Professional and Specialized Institutions	Maturation and proliferation of private universities, and state universities flourish with legislation such as the Morrill Act
Mass Higher Education	1960s–1980s	Includes traditional higher education and two-year colleges	Truman Commission Report
Postsecondary Education	1980s–1990s	Includes mass higher education and proprietary institutions	1972 Federal aid legislation, Vietnam veterans seek opportunities
Global Postsecondary Education and Training	2000 and beyond	Includes postsecondary education, for-profits, international institutions, corporate universities, and training companies	Evolving technologies, rising international economies and nations.

leges and universities to ignore the role that these nontraditional organizations, domestically and abroad, play or will play in the education and the development of human capital. International institutions as competitors to American colleges and universities are yet another influence forcing the evolution of the industry. Chinese and Indian higher education systems are quickly learning how to educate their own populations, which potentially affects the international student demand for American institutions. If American colleges and universities do not effectively recruit international students, some of the diversity and social fabric of their institutions will be lost. Most Chinese and Indian universities do not yet produce the same quality and caliber of education as their U.S. counterparts, but it would be a mistake to not consider them as legitimate contenders for qualified and motivated students in the coming years.

New industry players also come in forms that traditional colleges and universities have been slow to recognize. Corporations and private companies deliver training, education, or a mixture of the two. Such entrants into the higher education marketplace expand the boundaries of the traditional Postsecondary Education industry. As a consequence, universities can no longer discount the role that companies such as National Seminars Groups or the American Management Association play in delivering training and education in this new environment. Seminars, such as those offered by the Disney Institute and Ritz Carlton, offer curricula that contain combinations of skill acquisition (training) and educational development. Indeed, training and education are not mutually exclusive, and any organization, any place in the world, can provide either or both, to varying degrees. Players from the Postsecondary era advocate the need to improve traditional measures of educational attainment (e.g., associate or bachelor's degrees awarded), but Global Postsecondary Education and Training era competitors are providing real world knowledge and skills that shouldn't be viewed as exclusively short-term.

Technology also expands the industry. Technology enables new and existing industry players to disaggregate learning experiences and sell them through the Internet, in traditional classrooms, and in ways that are only beginning to materialize. Coaches, educators, and trainers not only occupy classrooms and hotel conferences, they travel to the student through the Internet or in person. The very nature of education, training, and learning continues to expand.

INDUSTRY ANALYSIS IN GLOBAL POSTSECONDARY EDUCATION AND TRAINING

An industry analysis is a big picture perspective of the environment, organizations, groups, and individuals that comprise it. Porter's (1980) framework has long been the standard on which industry analysis rests. Porter outlines five forces to consider in any industry: the threat of entrants, the intensity of the rivalry among existing players, the threat of substitutes for the existing products or services offered within the industry, the bargaining power of buyers, and the bargaining power of suppliers. All of these forces influence the success or failure of a given institution. Figure 1 displays the basic components of Porter's five-force industry analysis model.

An industry analysis for higher education can be created by region (e.g., eastern or southern United States), state (e.g., Ohio, Illinois, Indiana), sector (e.g., community colleges or regional four-year colleges), program offering (e.g., nursing, teacher preparation, or engineering), or even degree (e.g., Associate's or doctoral). As a starting point, the initial analysis in this chapter takes a broad perspective by explaining the five forces within the context of the Global Postsecondary Education and Training industry. This macro examination addresses the contextual parameters in which any state, institution, college, department, or program operates. The explanation of each force and the sources that define those forces draw on Porter's work but define them in terms relevant to higher education. The explanations that follow should be seen as a starting point for understanding the five

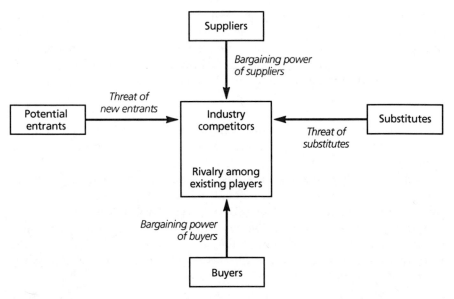

Figure 1 Porter's five forces.

forces. The five forces provide an initial framework to help colleges and universities understand their environment, but there may be additional forces that evolve and thus influence the dynamic higher education industry.

Threat of New Entrants

New or existing organizations can begin offering duplicate products or services to compete with what is already offered in any industry, including higher education. New entrants are defined by the similarity in what they offer compared to what already exists. For example, when community colleges propose to offer four-year degrees that compete with existing four-year degrees offered by universities, they pose a threat as a new entrant. The potential for a new entrant with a competing offering into the existing higher education marketplace depends on several factors: economies of scale, capital requirements, competitive advantage, reaction from existing competitors, and the level of buyer acceptance or resistance.

Each of the factors is discussed below except competitive advantage. A competitive advantage can come in the form of three different strategies: differentiation, cost advantage, or focus. Competitive advantage enhances the viability of potential entrants, or, when formulated by existing players, deters potential entrants. The area of competitive advantage is sufficiently developed such that it merits its own discussion, which is found in Chapter 6.

Economies of scale: Economies of scale refer to an organization's ability to increase productivity or decrease its average cost of production by more efficiently employing resources over time. If existing providers create economies of scale, then the threat of new entrants decreases; if existing providers do not create economies of scale, then the threat of new entrants increases. For example, if a college offers an entry-level math course in a lecture hall that seats one-hundred students but only enrolls fifty students, the college has excess capacity that it can put to use by filling the remaining fifty seats with students. There is little additional cost associated with such an action, and the college will realize economies of scale by doing so. The college can further reduce the average cost per student by hiring a teaching assistant instead of assigning a tenured professor to the course. It might be argued that increasing class size or hiring a teaching assistant increases efficiency at the expense of effectiveness. One hundred students in a classroom will not receive the quality of attention that fifty might; a teaching assistant might not be as effective as a tenured professor. These are all legitimate concerns. Because effectiveness is often an exercise in judgment and common sense and efficiency usually focuses on only those things we can measure, the key is to balance the two.

Economies of scale is a concept applicable to a classroom and an entire campus. The idea of "fully-funding" public colleges and universities illustrates perhaps the most blatant example of how administrators and academics ignore economies of scale and thus efficiency. Public community colleges and universities often argue that their states are not fully-funding their institutions. This argument almost always relies on a definition of a formula that promised years ago to fund each student at, say, $5,000 per year (plus a yearly inflation increase). The problem with this argument is that it ignores economies of scale. It is very expensive to educate the first student who comes through the door. The first student needs a building, a professor, and materials. But when ten more students enroll, these "fixed costs" are spread over a greater number of students. The marginal cost of each additional student is less than the one before. There comes a point where we have to erect new buildings and hire more professors, but until we reach that point, it is fairly naïve to claim that each additional student should be funded at exactly the same level as the last. Those who fail to recognize economies of scale are forever trapped in a quality/effectiveness versus efficiency argument whose only result is a stalemate.

Capital requirements: Capital requirements pertain to the monetary infrastructure investments needed to produce or deliver a product or service. In the technological world, it is possible to compete in the marketplace with relatively modest levels of capital investment, with the Google Corporation as a prime example. Although the world of higher education is different from the business world, higher education institutions are not immune from the very forces that propel private corporations to make changes.

One evident change in business and higher education is the need for physical capital. Traditional colleges and universities invest millions of dollars in classroom buildings, student centers, residence halls, laboratories, technological support systems, libraries, and athletics facilities. For-profit institutions have learned to minimize capital investment requirements by leasing building space and excluding expensive athletic and residential investments, which allows them to concentrate their efforts on academic offerings. Institutions that focus on online delivery, such as Capella University and Walden University, have further reduced physical capital requirements by only offering degree programs over the Internet. (A new organization offering a service that attempts to compete with an existing one, but in a different manner, is referred to as a substitute, which we address shortly). Capella and Walden Universities highlight how technological investment has in some instances replaced physical infrastructure and thus changed the cost structure of doing business.

High levels of any type of capital investment mean that new organizations are less likely to enter the industry. High investment requirements deter potential competitors in any industry. Consider the high levels of investment required to start an airline or residential college campus. In the airlines industry, high capital investment assures domination by a few large carriers. In higher education, the creation of a residential campus requires dormitories, dining halls, and all the traditional administrative, teaching, and research facilities. High capital investment requirements in physical infrastructure are precisely why there are few stories chronicling the opening of new campuses. In those cases where new colleges and universities are created, it is only through public support that such investment requirements can be met, such as in the University of California's newest campus at Merced.

Most new organizational forms that have emerged in the Global and Postsecondary Education and Training Industry have figured out how to minimize the exorbitant, physical capital investment requirements, much as the Google Corporations of the world have done in the technology industry. In the future, investment barriers of all kinds may be further minimized. Tapscott and Williams (2006) outline the seismic changes that collaboration in all industries is having on competitive advantage, and those leading our nation's institutions of higher education should take note. In a world where growing numbers of people collaborate to deliver any good and service, the entrenched interests that have prospered under prevailing entry barriers are threatened. Even the high cost of obtaining financial, physical, and human capital is becoming easier to overcome (Tapscott & Williams, 2006, p. 17).

Competitor reaction: Competitors often react negatively to new or potential entrants. This is true in business and education. Contrary to popular belief, private businesses do not embrace competition. Every private business, if it had its druthers, would operate as a monopoly and gladly accept government subsidies. A monopoly is more profitable than a marketplace full of competitors. In fact, private businesses do everything they can to convince politicians to pass state or federal legislation to benefit their organizations. Established higher education institutions behave in a similar manner. Consider the endless accounts across the states of university officials' negative reactions to community college proposals to offer select baccalaureates. A community college department offering a four-year degree usually means competition for a university. Similar dynamics occur when comprehensive universities propose to offer select doctoral programs. In fairness, some of the negative reaction to four-year offerings at community colleges or doctoral offerings at comprehensive universities relates to issues of duplication and efficient use of state resources, but the reaction from existing and established players is predictable and creates a barrier to entry for potential competitors.

Buyer resistance: Potential market entrants face two forms of buyer resistance: (1) a failure to accept the new product or service as equal to or better than existing products or services, or (2) an unwillingness to bear the costs of switching to the new product or service. Switching costs can be economic or psychological. The University of Phoenix is by any measure an illustration of a successful company, but it also demonstrates how the two forms of buyer resistance persist despite that success. Many adults seeking a master's degree still question whether employers view a master's degree from the University of Phoenix as equivalent to a master's degree from a traditional university campus. Students who seek a master's degree as a stepping stone into a doctoral program are especially skeptical of obtaining a master's degree from the University of Phoenix, as faculty in traditional doctoral programs often hold negative perceptions about these degrees. Finally, the University of Phoenix charges a premium for its programs, and thus the switching costs, when combined with perceptions about quality, increase the costs of switching from a public university program to the University of Phoenix.

Intensity of Rivalry

The intensity of rivalry among existing players in the higher education industry manifests itself in the competition for students, faculty, research money, donor contributions, and state funds. It is greatly influenced by two structural factors: the profile of the existing players and industry context. Institutional actions, such as the creation of institutional scholarships or new recruitment efforts, are simply the byproducts of a competitive industry environment. Such actions should ideally take place based on knowledge of the environmental context. It is easy to get caught up in the short-term tactics that appear to increase competitiveness. For example, some nonprofit colleges now spend significant amounts of money on Internet-based marketing strategies to attract more students. The institutions are charged for the number of "hits" that are generated from the marketing effort. Colleges using these "pay-per-click" campaigns find that Internet providers have increased prices over the last several years (Blumenstyk, 2006). Clearly, a marketing campaign such as this is a reaction to the perceived competitiveness and market conditions of the industry, but at what cost? The integration of the structural factors of rivalry into industry analysis provides a more informed perspective on anticipated results versus costs. This perspective can help determine what actions, behaviors, and maybe even marketing campaigns, are appropriate.

Profile of existing players: The profile of existing players in a given higher education market is defined by the number and type of institutions within the industry. This profile determines the degree to which each of the players must engage in competitive actions for students, faculty, research money, donor contributions, and state funds.

The profile of existing players usually exists somewhere along the continuum of two extremes: domination by a handful of institutions or a diverse mix of players. Where only a handful of institutions dominate a given market, the need for competitive action is minimized. If an institution is the only "game in town," it would make little sense to expend precious resources on tactical actions that will likely produce marginal returns. If, for purposes of analysis, we define a particular state as a potential higher education market, large public research institutions in several western and Midwestern states hold a dominate position in the industry. States such as Arizona, Nevada, New Mexico, and Oklahoma do not have a significant number of private institutions that compete with public institutions for students. The state higher education industry in these states is, by most measures, dominated by public institutions. In the case of Arizona and New Mexico, the combination of population growth and general propensity of the college age population to resist out-state migration ensures a steady stream of enrollment demand for top state public research institutions. If Arizona and New Mexico public research universities expand their market space beyond their respective states and compete for out-of-state and international students, then the profile of existing players and therefore intensity of rivalry changes.

The profile of existing higher education players in most eastern states is quite different from that found in western states. In Massachusetts, more students attend private than public institutions. New York's private sector is substantial, and the state of New Jersey even provides some level of funding to private universities. In Pennsylvania, there also is a diverse mix of institutions, all competing for students and resources in a climate of a stagnant and even declining population base. Such conditions increase the intensity of rivalry and necessitate the consideration of a second structural factor, the influence of industry context on industry growth.

The influence of industry context on industry growth: The context in which higher education operates is defined by political, economic, social and technological (PEST) variables. This context presents opportunities and threats, and an institution's ability to act on the former and avert the latter depends on its strengths and weaknesses (SWOT). Although the PEST and SWOT analyses were introduced in the strategic planning chapter, they are not exclusive components of strategic planning but can inform multiple approaches to strategy making.

The political and economic contexts of the higher education industry are intricately connected, especially when considering public institutions. Funding for state public higher education is, in large part, driven by available tax revenues, which are in turn influenced by a state's economic climate. In times of fiscal austerity, political choices dictate the extent to which higher education is funded. Although no analysis can predict long-term economic patterns with certainty, any strategy must account for, to the extent possible, the economic climate.

Demographic shifts are a largely predictable social force. As discussed in Chapter 3, demographic growth can point to an opportunity to capture a growing market share while demographic decline can indicate a threat to the institution's current service offerings and thus signal that a shift in emphasis might be necessary.

Finally, technological trends and discoveries dramatically influence the intensity of rivalry in any industry. In higher education, technological innovation has influenced rivalry on both the teaching and research fronts. Those institutions that capitalize on technological innovation and discovery enhance their competitive position as they move to the forefront of teaching and research.

Threat of Substitutes

Pines and Gilmore (1999) speak of the experience economy, and how consumers of all types seek experiences. In the traditional sense, higher education institutions have always provided an experience. One "experiences" higher education over a number of years. Indeed, the reason why colleges and universities have survived centuries is largely because higher education has always created unparalleled lifetime experiences for students. Those who experience it want the same for their children.

The college experience is most affiliated with the traditional residential campus, but the higher education industry has expanded because new organizational forms have emerged to meet changing needs. Organizations such as community colleges and proprietary schools became legitimate substitutes for traditional institutions with the evolution of the postsecondary era. Today, online programs promote themselves as alternatives to their traditional counterparts. These alternatives are substitute services, and they are different, in some way, from the existing ones. Substitutes compete with and provide alternatives to existing services.

In higher education, the mode of course delivery often distinguishes a substitute offering. For instance, if the offering makes significant use of technology relative to existing delivery avenues, or reduces the time it takes to complete the course, then it is distinct enough to qualify as a substitute rather than a new entrant (a duplicate offering). To be sure, many of the factors that enable new entrants to penetrate existing markets, such as lower investment requirements or failure to capitalize on economies of scale, also give substitute offerings increased viability. In the case of substitutes, consumers must, over time, judge whether that substitute provides an acceptable level of service compared to the service that existing suppliers provide.

Substitute offerings in higher education do not just emanate from existing institutions that want to expand their services. If players from the Postsecondary Education era do not yet consider training companies and corporate universities as direct competitors, then they must at least consider them as potential substitutes. Identifying substitutes, or potential substitutes, for existing higher education services is a matter of examining the learning experience in terms of three parameters: convenience, time, and application. If a substitute service fares well on these three parameters, then it is likely to be seen as having similar or equivalent functionality to that which already exists.

Time: Time is one of the most important factors driving those who seek higher education services to consider substitutes. Many people do not want to invest four or five years to obtain a bachelor's degree. Professionals seeking credentials that will help them qualify for pay raises or advancement are not willing to take the two years required to complete a traditional Master's degree.

The time element has been greatly influenced by demographic shifts. Adult students constitute a larger segment of the student market than ever before. Adult students aged twenty-five and above differed greatly from the traditional 18-22 year-old college student. Adult students typically work full-time, have family responsibilities, and are willing to forego the traditional college experience. For-profit institutions have produced degree offerings that decrease the time it takes to earn that degree. Seminar and training companies have "modularized" education and training topics to such an extent that certain knowledge and skill attainment is often possible in one to five days. Are providers who cut the time that it takes to acquire the education and training creating legitimate substitutes? Based on the growth of the for-profit sector and continued sustainability of the seminar and training industry, the answer seems to be yes.

Convenience: Convenience, like time, is largely a response to consumer demand for education and training delivered at times and in ways that are customized to their needs. Evening and weekend courses are now common. Module offerings over the Internet, which can be viewed at any time, are also available. Podcasts offer yet another alternative to the standard, place-and-time bound classroom lecture. Those organizations that seek to maximize education and training for the customized convenience of the student may soon find their substitutes becoming industry standards.

Application: The philosophical debates about the importance of a liberal arts education seems, in many respects, to have given way to the practicality of higher education as a means to economic success. Indeed, Astin's (1997) thirty-year summary of his annual survey of freshmen found that students' motivations for seeking higher education became increasingly economic in nature compared to years earlier, when they were more interested in developing a meaningful philosophy of life. More recent survey results have fluctuated slightly, but overall the trend toward the interest in higher education as a financial rather than a philosophical means remains. Today, consumers who invest in education and training want knowledge and skills that are marketable and lead to good jobs, which in turn signifies an economic return that justifies the consumer's monetary investment in education and training.

Interestingly, it is not just students who are driven by application over theory. The rise of application-based research, often protected by patents, licenses, and copyrights, has major implications for higher education's role in society as a knowledge producer. Instead of knowledge for the public, which is disseminated freely to the public, discoveries by application-based researchers often remain proprietary. For many universities, application-based research has emerged as a legitimate substitute for theory-based research. Institutions that pursue application-based research compete for federal and private monies as well as national prominence.

The combination of time, convenience, and application in the student market: Competitors who offer substitutes often combine convenience, time, and application, largely because of expanded delivery options made possible via technology. Entire institutions are offered online. Community colleges, state colleges, and research universities offer courses, certificates, programs, and degrees online. The extent to which these online offerings make use of technology relative to existing offerings may distinguish them enough to qualify as substitute services.

Arizona State University (ASU), for example, offers an online corporate MBA program designed specifically for employees at the Deere Company in Moline, Illinois. ASU's main campus is located in Phoenix, Arizona. This program competes directly for students with the MBA program at Western Illinois University, which is physically located in the Moline area. Over time, Deere management has perceived little or no difference in the quality of the two offerings. The Deere Company sees merit in its employees receiving courses tailored to the firm's needs, and the employees view one MBA as good as another. Both management and employees value ease of access and their ability to determine when and where the program is delivered. Convenience, alone, makes the tradeoff of substantially higher costs for the ASU program worth the investment, from Deere's perspective.

Today's substitute providers often become major industry players tomorrow, directly competing with established organizations. As substitute services morph into direct competition, they also hold the potential to redefine the industry. The many forces that influence the higher education industry and its subsequent evolution are certain to be affected by the combination of time, convenience, and application.

Bargaining Power of Buyers

Buyers of a service are synonymous with customers. Students (and their parents) are customers in the sense that they buy an education from an institution. The federal government is a customer when it buys research services from a university. In perfect markets, buyers have perfect information and plentiful choices. An industry marked by perfect information and plentiful choices means that industry rivalry is high, since a number of organizations compete for customers who are well informed and have choices. Higher education is not a perfect market, and information and choice are two parameters by which to analyze the bargaining power that buyers do have. More information and choice increase the bargaining power of the buyers.

Information: Information allows buyers to compare services, in terms of quality, breadth of offerings, and numerous other features. In higher education, accrediting agencies, state governments, and third parties, such as *U.S. News and World Report* and *The Financial Times,* provide information on higher education institutions and the services they render. Accreditation has long played the role of validating the quality of higher education programs. Law schools, for example, that are not accredited by the American Bar Association are at a significant competitive disadvantage in the industry, as their programs are not perceived to have equivalent value to those programs that are accredited. In general, graduates of accredited programs have more career options than graduates of unaccredited programs. Many rankings of national programs will not even include unaccredited programs in their tabulations. By this count, unaccredited programs miss an opportunity to build brand recognition because they cannot take advantage of free press about the value of their offerings.

Third parties, such as *U.S. News and World Report,* consistently publish information about institutions and their programs. The published information from these sources is perhaps the best circulated among the general public. Although some critics within higher education condemn the validity of the measures used to assess institutions and programs, few argue that potential students and employers pay attention to such information. Entire institutions base their strategic efforts on improving their standing in popular journal rankings. Baylor University developed a 10-year strategic plan, Baylor 2012, with an overarching goal to enter the top tier of institutions, as determined by *U.S. News and World Report's* college rankings (Farrell & Van der Werf, 2007).

Institutions also make information available about themselves, in print and over the Internet. Institutions promote themselves in the best possible manner with self-published material, which potential students access for information about programs, research endeavors, student life, and faculty. The 'ideal' characteristics of one institution are compared with another institution at the click of a button, giving potential students more information by which to make their choices.

Choice: Choice is inextricably tied to the profile of industry players. In an industry where options are plentiful, customers have more choice and thus buyer power increases. A certain level of competition is usually desirable because competitors tend to be more sensitive to inputs and feedback from those they serve. In some higher education markets, there exists a rich array of institutional types. Students that do not want to attend one institution, or perhaps are unable to meet the requirements of a particular institution, have other choices. New York City is an example of an area with a rich diversity of institutions, ranging from world class, private elite universities to specialized culinary institutes. Where there are few institutions or institutional types, buyer power is limited. In several states, buyer power is reduced because the higher education market is dominated by public institutions that act more as monopolies than service organizations. Few private colleges and universities exist, so competition is limited, which limits buyer power. In the state of Michigan, for example, public four-year institutions dominate the market and account for almost 50% of total higher education enrollments in the state. In total, two and four-year public institution enrollment is more than 80% of the market (Chronicle of Higher Education

Almanac, 2005–6). Student choice is limited in Michigan compared to New York City.

Buyer power does not just apply to student choice. The federal government also buys higher education services. By awarding research grants through its various departments, the federal government in essence buys research services from colleges and universities. The federal government's power in purchasing research services is extremely high because there are many researchers and institutions from which to choose. The competition among universities that want to provide research services is very keen, and no major university provides more than a fraction of the services the federal government purchases. In terms of purchasing research services, the federal government as buyer operates in a very competitive marketplace.

Bargaining Power of Suppliers

In industry analysis, suppliers are defined as those organizations or individuals who provide the materials, information, or knowledge that allow an organization to produce its products and services. Farmers supply the beans for Starbuck's coffee just as steel companies furnish raw material for the automobile industry. A supplier's power is linked to competition, the importance of the supplier to the organization or industry it services, and the availability of substitute products. If numerous farmers compete to sell beans to Starbuck's, then supplier power decreases. If only a few steel companies can provide the raw materials that Ford needs to build cars, then supplier power increases.

In higher education, suppliers might include all of those organizations that supply auxiliary services that one finds at an institution. Bookstores, health clinics, and food services all offer services that one finds within the operation of an institutional campus. Yet, these suppliers are only complementary to the core services of teaching, research, and service. Porter (1980, p. 28) states that we usually think of suppliers as other organizations, but labor must be recognized as a supplier as well. Labor should be conceived of as an important supplier particularly for organizations and industries where said labor is highly skilled or very influential in the delivery of the goods or services under consideration.

Hospitals and universities represent organizations in which labor should be viewed through the lens of supplier. Doctors and faculty are highly specialized, highly educated, and work with great independence and autonomy in the delivery of their expertise. In higher education, the faculty constitutes a major operating expenditure for an institution. Non-academic support staff constitutes another potential supplier group within the higher education industry. The undifferentiated nature of qualifications required between this group and the relatively high numbers of individuals who can assume these roles, however, precludes it from possessing significant power.

The power of faculty as supplier varies depending on institutional type and discipline. Faculty at traditional four-year research universities work under conditions of great discretion and autonomy, protected by tenure systems as they exercise judgment and academic freedom in teaching and research. But even within traditional universities, there are relative degrees of power. Faculty at elite private, research universities are the most powerful suppliers in the industry. Many professors at these institutions are among the best-known contributors to their fields and as such are not easily replaced given their reputations and high levels of expertise. Public university faculty enjoys similar status as those at private institutions, but, in general, not to the same degree. Tenured faculty at public and private research universities also hold considerable power simply because the fate of their jobs is largely out of the control of those who manage the institutions for which they work.

Faculty at comprehensive universities, community colleges, proprietary schools, and for-profit institutions also hold a degree of power as suppliers to the industry, but considerably less than their research university counterparts. Community colleges typically hire fewer faculty with doctoral degrees than do universities, thus the pool from which to select labor is more extensive than what is available for a research university. In addition, community colleges, technical schools, and for-profit institutions make liberal use of adjunct faculty, which equates to a flexible labor force with reduced supplier power. If faculty is unionized, whether in a community college or any other type of institution, then supplier power increases.

The supplier power of faculty not only varies by institutional type but also by discipline. In some fields, such as history and English, more qualified faculty than positions exist, thereby decreasing supplier power, particularly at the front end of the hiring process. In contrast, there are few Ph.D.s in finance. An individual with a Ph.D. in finance has greater supplier power than the individual with a Ph.D. in history. Porter's industry analysis framework is economic in nature, and therefore the forces of supply and demand ultimately determine the bargaining power of buyers and suppliers.

Government as the Sixth Force

Porter's classic framework identifies five forces that determine industry competition: the threat of new entrants, the intensity of the rivalry among existing players, the threat of substitutes for the existing products or services offered within the industry, the bargaining power of buyers, and the bargaining power of suppliers. Porter (1980) does mention that government might also be a legitimate force in the industry: "... government at all levels must be recognized as potentially influencing many if not all aspects of industry structure both directly and indirectly. In many industries, government is a buyer and supplier and can influence industry competition by the policies that it adopts." (p. 28). Federal, state, and local governments may be a part of or an influence on any of the five forces in the higher education industry.

The federal government acts as a buyer by purchasing research from higher education, but governmental influence extends well beyond this activity. Federal and state governments also furnish student aid, increasing buyer bargaining power for the student. The availability of federal or state aid means students have expanded choices. A student who previously could not afford to attend a private university might now be able to make new and different choices.

Federal and state governments also provide information about higher education to help consumers make better choices. State governments also monitor public institutions and use accountability policies to measure outcomes. The accountability information that state governments generate, safeguards public values such as educational quality and access. The federal government also collects information from colleges, universities, and other postsecondary institutions regarding enrollments, completion rates, and costs. This information is publicly available and finds its way to research and media outlets that inform potential and existing buyers.

Similarly state and local governments influence industry rivalry by directly funding higher education institutions. Entire institutions are built, closed, or redefined; new degree programs created; and faculty (suppliers) paid more competitive wages based on the availability of government funding. The various government levels influence the higher education industry by empowering consumers, funding institutions, buying research, and disseminating information about colleges and universities. One normally perceives government involvement as stifling market mechanisms. In higher education, government might expand the market, create it, enable it, or limit it. Whatever the case, government is without question, the sixth force in the higher education industry.

A COMPREHENSIVE INDUSTRY ANALYSIS
OF HIGHER EDUCATION

An industry analysis helps create a comprehensive picture of the forces that shape an industry. In higher education, institutional or system strategy is best crafted when decision makers understand the context in which their organizations operate. Porter's framework provides a template by which to view the six forces of the higher education industry. Figure 2 tailors Porter's framework and provides a general industry analysis of higher education.

The general industry analysis in Figure 2 serves as a template that individual institutions, colleges, or programs can use to create a unit-level analysis of their industries. In the next chapter, we operationalize the six-forces industry analysis framework at the unit level.

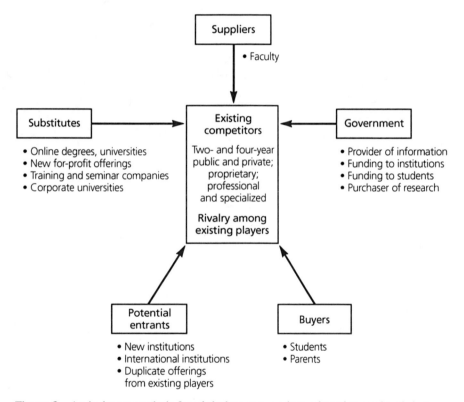

Figure 2 An industry analysis for global postsecondary education and training.

CHAPTER 5

APPLYING INDUSTRY ANALYSIS IN HIGHER EDUCATION

The Global Postsecondary and Training industry analysis from Chapter 4 is a broad macro view of the many forces that affect higher education institutions. A macro industry analysis provides a systemic view that helps an organization understand the forces that influence it directly and indirectly. Industry analysis is useful as an application tool if the organization or unit (states, institutions, colleges, or programs) constructing a strategy delimits its analysis to the most immediate and direct forces that influence its behaviors and operations. One way to delimit an industry analysis is to identify what are called strategic groups.

STRATEGIC GROUPS IN HIGHER EDUCATION

Competitive analysis makes use of what are called strategic groups. A strategic group is a set of organizations in an industry that competes across similar strategic dimensions (Grant, 2005, p. 124). A strategic dimension is often a characterization that says something about the product or service offering or the range of buyers the organization hopes to reach. Some organizations offer a variety of products or services intended to reach a global audience, others purposely limit their offerings and focus on local or regional markets. Hunt (1972) created the term in his analysis of the

Innovative Strategy Making in Higher Education, pages 63–73
Copyright © 2009 by Information Age Publishing
All rights of reproduction in any form reserved.

appliance industry. The concept evolved when Porter (1980) applied it to his strategic analysis, since different groups comprise an industry. The concept of strategic groups has primarily been applied to business and industry, largely because the analysis of strategic groups provides a way to view an organization vis-à-vis its competition. The relative position of one organization compared to others within the same industry and across multiple dimensions reveals insight about where competitive opportunities exist, or conversely, where there is excessive competition. In the automobile industry, for example, there are a range of providers. Some automakers primarily focus on markets in the country in which they reside, with a limited number of offerings. The Morgan Motor Company in the U.K. produces hand built, quality vehicles for auto enthusiasts. The company is not a mass production assembly-line operation, so it is unlikely that it will ever achieve a globally significant presence. In contrast, the product range for companies like Ford and Nissan is very broad because these organizations mass produce cars, trucks, SUVs, and minivans. Ford and Nissan are global in scope, because they produce a range of products and aim to sell them internationally.

The strategic group concept can also be applied to the higher education industry. Figure 3 is a picture of strategic groups within the Global Postsecondary Education and Training Industry. The figure is an extension of Table 2, from Chapter 4, and includes traditional institutions from the higher education industry as well as nontraditional organizations, such as corporate universities and training companies. The distinction between tra-

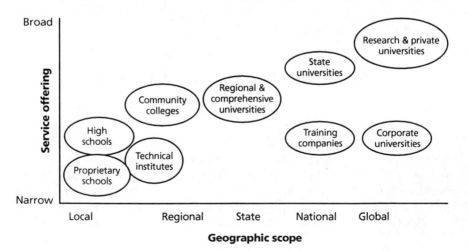

Figure 3 Strategic groups in the global postsecondary industry.

ditional and nontraditional providers of education and training is blurring, and Table 2 and Figure 3 recognize this reality.

Strategic groups are commonly depicted along two dimensions. Figure 3 shows a number of strategic groups (or providers) in the Global Postsecondary Education and Training Industry, as they exist across two strategic dimensions. The first strategic dimension is the range of Service Offerings that a strategic group might offer or provide. Some organizations offer a narrow range of education and training courses and services, whereas other providers seek a market that is global in scope. Technical and proprietary institutes tend to have limited service offerings because they focus on specific training skills. Consider cosmetology schools, which specialize in hair, nail, and skin care but do not offer education or training in subjects such as English or mathematics. The cosmetology school's service offerings are limited because it hopes to create very specific job opportunities for those who complete certificates.

High schools, in at least some ways, are part of the Global Postsecondary Education and Training Industry because many of them offer advanced placement courses in a range of subjects, which count toward college credit. Major research universities have very broad educational service offerings relative to other providers shown in the figure. Technically, and quite literally, research universities are charged with investigating and offering everything conceivable in the universe. The range of colleges, programs, courses, and student services (which are part of the educational experience) under one university umbrella is so vast that administrators are essentially managing multimillion or even multibillion dollar conglomerate businesses. Students at universities engage in a variety of study programs, ranging from pop culture to agricultural economics. Regional universities and community colleges are usually not as expansive in their service offerings as their research university counterparts. Therefore, they fall in the middle of the Service Offering strategic dimension.

The second strategic dimension shown on the horizontal axis in Figure 3 is the Geographic Scope of the organization. Geographic Scope refers to what is called impact and reach. Impact is the effect the organization has on its environment through its activity and service offerings. Reach has more to do with the market from which the organization hopes to draw. Large corporate universities serve employees around the world so are global in scope. McDonald's University and Motorola University provide specific education and training to employees. Even though their service offerings are not expansive, their reach and impact are. Employees receive training and education and then return to apply their newly acquired skills to the various locations in which they reside.

Most traditional educational organizations follow a pattern when it comes to reach and impact: those that hope to impact a given geographic area also recruit students that are representative of that area (reach). Policy makers and community leaders often view community colleges as very responsive to local needs because these institutions focus on recruiting, educating, training, and retraining for students and citizens of their communities. Community colleges are nimble, and they can develop programs that respond to the business and industry needs of organizations in their area. For all of these reasons, the geographic scope of community colleges is local and/or regional in nature. The University of Pennsylvania (Penn), by contrast, is a major research university with educational and research endeavors that are global in scope. Penn attracts national and international student applicants. The research and writing that is produced by faculty at the institution have also had an impact on a global scale, with notable contributions in fields as diverse as finance, medical research, and speech communications.

The strategic groups lens affords the strategist an intriguing perspective into the Global Postsecondary Education and Training Industry. It is here that the strategist views the span of competition, the activities and actions that define that competition, and how one's own organization fits within that broad population. The concept of strategic groups as an analytical tool is meant to be flexible, and the leader can create a refined view of a limited number of strategic groups or a more sweeping picture of an entire industry. For instance, a comprehensive state university may wish to eliminate any research universities from its analysis, hence limiting the number of strategic groups and focusing its strategy analysis on only other regional universities, community colleges, and proprietary institutions. Delimitations usually reduce the scope of the strategic dimensions as well. The national and global components of the geographic scope dimension become less important for a comprehensive university that chooses to eliminate research universities from its analysis.

Strategy groups, however they are defined, provide a picture of the industry in which a particular institution operates. The dynamic interaction among strategy groups and the dimensions along which they compete influences the intensity of competition, the threat of new entrants, the threat of substitutes, the bargaining power of buyers and suppliers, and the actions and reactions of government. The strategy groups that are included in a given analysis also influence how one defines each of these six forces or answers questions related to each force.

IDENTIFYING YOUR COMPETITION
USING INDUSTRY ANALYSIS

The next six sections provide application templates for each of the six-forces comprising the higher education industry. Chapter 4 presented various factors associated with each force, and the application templates contain questions pertaining to these same factors. The application templates raise questions to help a strategic unit (state, institution, college, or program) understand its macro environment and the forces that influence organizational success and failure. For those wishing to obtain a more revealing analysis, we recommend formally defining strategic groups prior to answering the questions in the templates. From this perspective, the templates help profile the immediate forces and players that influence organizational performance within a specific set of strategic groups. If the strategic groups are unclear, institutional leaders will find that the very process of discussing the application questions helps define its competing strategic groups.

The application questions serve as a guide to help units initiate discussion about the forces that increase competitive pressure or present opportunities or threats. Most colleges and universities already know something about themselves if they have engaged in the rigors of strategic planning. The questions in the templates build on the knowledge base that might have already been laid through the strategic planning process. Applying industry analysis at the unit level, through the lens of the six forces, reveals information about that unit's own resources and capabilities, key aspects of the strategy groups with which it identifies, and details about the competitive environment in which it lives.

The Threat of New Entrants

Economies of scale, capital requirements, and competitive advantage (differentiation, focus, and cost advantage) all influence the extent to which new entrants will be drawn to a particular segment of the higher education industry. Table 3 breaks down each of these factors, summarizes the impact of the factor on competition, and asks application questions that should be discussed in the process of creating a more comprehensive strategy.

A number of general questions also arise regarding potential competitors. The questions below can serve as an impetus to help a strategy team think about how it defines the evolving industry or strategy group of which they are a part. Conjecture may drive some of the answers to the questions,

TABLE 3   Threat of New Entrants: Factors and Questions

Factor	Impact on Competition	Application Questions
Economies of scale	Decreases competition if economies of scale realized	• Does your institution purposely pursue efficiencies? • Where might you increase efficiency without sacrificing quality? • Do faculty and staff (in particular departments or areas) have experience that can be used to increase efficiency without sacrificing quality? • Do you make appropriate use of adjunct and part-time workers?
Capital requirements	Decreases competition if capital requirements are high	• Have capital, human, or technological investment requirements increased or decreased in your strategy group? • Do you have existing or incoming resources to invest? • Are you losing resources?
Differentiation	Decreases competition if differentiation is high	Discussion in Chapter 6
Cost disadvantage	Decreases competition if there are high investment costs to enter the market	Discussion in Chapter 6

but the organization's own unconscious assumptions are what will likely surface as a result of the discussion.

- Who are our potential competitors?
- What assumptions do we hold about each potential competitor?
- What is each potential competitor doing now and/or capable of doing (current strategies)?
- What are each potential competitor's strengths and weaknesses?
- What are we mistakenly doing to encourage potential competitors to enter our market space?
- What can we do to discourage potential competitors from entering our market space?
- If one of these potential competitors offered a new but duplicate service (e.g., new program), would it be viable?

Intensity of the Rivalry

Influential factors that contribute to the intensity of industry rivalry include the profile of existing players and the industry context. Table 4 breaks down each of these factors, summarizes the impact of the factor on competition, and asks application questions that should be discussed in the process of creating a more comprehensive strategy. The questions in Table 4 provide a comprehensive discussion guide.

If possible, systematically surveying students who applied for admission, were admitted, and subsequently did not enroll provides another perspective on one's closest competitors. These questions can be directed at the institution, college, department, or program level. Surveying current students may be more practical. Current students can provide information about the strengths of your institution.

- Why did you choose to attend this institution?
- What was the most important reason for not attending another institution?
- What other alternatives did you consider?

TABLE 4   Intensity of Rivalry: Factors and Questions

Factor	Impact on Competition	Application Questions
Profile of existing players	Variable	• What is the mix of public versus private and two- versus four-year institutions in what you consider your market space? • What are the most popular programs offered by most competitive players? • Where do you, or customers, perceive the strengths of your competitors?
Context	Variable	• What are the demographics with respect to age and ethnicity of your target student population? • Is the short-term state and federal economic outlook positive or negative? • Does the state tax structure allow sufficient revenue collections for public institutions? • Is technological delivery an accepted mode of delivery for your target customers? Is it expected?

- What didn't you like about each alternative?
- If possible, ask students enrolled at other institutions:
- What was the most important reason for attending your institution?
- What was the most important reason for not attending our institution?

The Threat of Substitutes

Factors that contribute to the threat of substitutes include time, convenience, and application. Table 5 breaks down each of these factors, summarizes the potential for substitutes relative to the factors, and asks application questions that should be discussed in the process of creating a more informed strategy.

Bargaining Power of Buyers

Information and choice are the primary factors that determine buyer power. Table 6 breaks down each of these factors, summarizes the impact of the factor on competition, and asks application questions that should be discussed in the process of creating a more comprehensive strategy.

TABLE 5   Threat of Substitutes: Factors and Questions

Factor	Potential for Substitutes	Application Questions
Time	Increases if substitute service provider is able to decrease time to degree or decrease the time it takes to deliver the service	• Is there potential to decrease your service delivery time? • If your service delivery time is longer than a potential substitute's time, have you deliberately communicated why this is the case, to your customers? • Have you communicated the benefits of your time to delivery?
Convenience	Increases if substitute service provider is able to increase convenience of delivery, or customize the delivery, to the buyer	• Have you used technology to enhance customization and convenience to your market, without sacrificing quality? • Have you accounted for your customer's schedules and preferences?
Application	Increases if substitute service provider is able to convince the market that the delivery of service will result in direct, profitable, and personal application	• What is the appropriate balance and/or intersection between education and skills based applications, from your perspective? How does the answer to this question affect your ability to compete?

TABLE 6   Bargaining Power of Buyers: Factors and Questions

Factor	Impact on Competition	Application Questions
Information	More information increases buyer power	• Does the information you put out, in its many forms (Internet, pamphlets, etc.), send a consistent message so as to properly brand your institution? • Do you have evidence that the information you disseminate is reaching the target market? • Do you have evidence that the information you disseminate is having the intended effect?
Choice	More choice increases buyer power	Same application questions as for Profile of Existing Players: • What is the mix of public versus private and two- versus four-year institutions in what you consider your market space? • What are the most popular programs offered by the most competitive players? • Where do you, or customers, perceive the strengths of your competitors?

The Bargaining Power of Suppliers

Faculty (suppliers) have a sense of what potential students look for in a school or program because they talk to them and, to some extent, know where students apply for admission. Because institutions are organized by discipline, faculties are connected to colleagues in their discipline across institutions. Therefore, often faculties are the best source for understanding other institutions in terms of their teaching, research, and service attributes. Program faculty should be included in discussions that ask the following questions:

- What institutions and programs are primary competitors to our institution and its programs?
- What draws students to our competitors?
- What draws faculty to our competitors?
- What draws research monies to our competitors?

The Power of Government

The higher education industry is influenced by federal, state and even local government. Government at all levels uses financial and legislative tools to structure or restructure the existing industry. Table 7 highlights

TABLE 7 Power of Government: Factors and Questions

Force	Effect on Industry	Application Questions
Federal government	Increases competition and market-like conditions by distributing financial aid and federal grants	• What percentage of our funding comes from research or service grants? • How much do our students receive in total federal aid per student? Pell grants per student? Loans per student?
State government	Influences industry structure through state-level aid and through state-level governance. The effect of influence is variable depending on the nature of aid and governance structure.	• Does state governance allow for more autonomy or greater regulation? How has it changed? Is it going to change in the future? • How much do our students receive in total state aid per student? State grants per student? • How has state funding changed over the last five years, in terms of absolute dollars? • What proportion of our current revenue is comprised of state funding? Last year? Five years ago?
Local government	Typically can increase the competitiveness of community colleges by providing operating and capital funding.	• How has local funding changed over the last five years, in terms of absolute dollars? • What proportion of our revenues is comprised of local funding today? Last year? Five years ago?

some questions that institutions should ask, just to develop a conscious understanding of how government at these three levels might influence industry structure.

CONCLUSION

An industry analysis provides a contextual view of an organization's environment and the various forces that comprise it. It reveals information about potential entrants, the intensity of rivalry, the potential for substitutions, the power of buyers and suppliers, and the influence of government. An industry analysis also provides clues about future events that are important to the organization's survival. Clearly, an industry analysis is an asset to the strategist's toolkit. A comprehensive industry analysis may indeed point to particular strategies that might be effective as higher education institutions compete in an increasingly dynamic and complex industry.

Chapter 4 provided the conceptual foundation upon which the industry analysis is built. Chapter 5 provided the templates that help bring that analysis to life by aligning the forces and factors with specific application questions. The application questions are the starting point to encourage discussion, which can lead to (a) additional discussion, or (b) specific strategies that the unit can implement in its competitive arena. The subject of the next chapter concerns the latter point. Its aim is to outline several specific strategies—competitive strategies—that can help higher education units position themselves for the future, given the industry, their organizational resources and capabilities, and their purpose and direction.

CHAPTER 6

EXERCISING YOUR COMPETITIVE ADVANTAGE

Once a college, university, or program has identified its current and potential competitors, understands the demands of its buyers and suppliers, and has calculated the extent to which government intervention determines the way it does business, it can begin to formulate strategies that will help it cope with the environmental and competitive constraints under which it must function. Organizations that seek a competitive advantage employ one or more of three generic strategies (Porter, 1985): cost leadership, differentiation, and focus. Niche development and market segmentation, terms readily used in business, are variants of the more generic focus strategy and as such are subsumed within this chapter. A fourth competitive strategy, integration, is distinct enough from the three strategies covered in this chapter that we devote Chapter 7 to its examination.

COST LEADERSHIP

Cost leadership refers to providing a product or service for a broad market at a given level of quality for the lowest price (Porter, 1985). Conversely, price can be used to convey quality, but this would not fall within the realm of a cost leadership strategy. Elite private universities like Columbia and Northwestern use price (high tuition) to signal superior quality and do not

Innovative Strategy Making in Higher Education, pages 75–89
Copyright © 2009 by Information Age Publishing
75

worry about being the cost leader. Maintaining the lowest price for the product or service, industry wide, exemplifies a true cost leadership strategy.

An organization achieves cost leadership by aggressively monitoring costs, employing economies of scale, hiring cheaper labor, avoiding the provision of high ticket services that might be associated with similar product/service offerings, and by operating out of facilities featuring few architectural or employee amenities. Public higher education institutions typically employ some degree of cost leadership strategies, simply because they are subsidized by their state governments. For instance, the University of California, Berkeley and Stanford University are both located in the San Francisco area, and both institutions have world class reputations and offer highly reputable academic programs. However, because UC-Berkeley is publicly supported, its in-state tuition is approximately a third of what it costs to enter Stanford. Further, for many majors, the quality in both universities is very high, meaning Berkeley is the hands-down cost leader for California residents, when viewed from this perspective.

Cost leadership strategies are not only evident when we compare public with private for-profit and not-for-profit universities, but they also play out across public institutional types. Community colleges charge lower tuition than four-year state colleges, and four-year colleges, in most instances, charge less than research universities. In Los Angeles, California State University-Los Angeles (CSU-LA), the University of California-Los Angeles (UCLA), and the Los Angeles Community College District are state-supported providers of publicly funded postsecondary education. Each offers the first two years of undergraduate education, but because their missions differ, the tuition charged mirrors their operating costs. The community colleges and CSU-LA do not offer costly doctoral programs, and their faculty, for the most part, do not engage in labor intensive research that requires substantial subsidies for laboratory equipment, space, and time. As a consequence, based on 2007 tuition levels, the first two years of undergraduate education costs less at the community college ($1,200) than at CSU-LA ($5,040) or at UCLA ($10,816).

Public community colleges provide the clearest example of cost leadership strategies for the first two-years of undergraduate education. Although they compete directly with in-state public universities for entering students, they employ a cost leadership strategy by maintaining larger class sizes, delivering courses online, employing fewer more costly full-time faculty, and often making generous use of adjunct faculty. In 2006 the Maricopa County Community College District served more than 250,000 students through classes offered by 1,300 full-time and 4,000 adjunct faculty. Arizona State University (ASU), which also serves the Phoenix metropolitan area, offers course work to 63,000 undergraduate and graduate students through 2,471 full and 391 part-time faculty. Some of its 2,500 graduate assistants also teach classes; even so, the ratio of students to full-time faculty is considerable higher within the community college system than at ASU.

In addition, community college facilities can be rather Spartan, which makes them inexpensive to build and easy to maintain. Community colleges rarely offer on-campus housing (a cost savings not only in capital expenditures but in staffing and maintenance as well) and often limit on-campus student services and activities. For instance, although some community colleges have competitive collegiate football teams, many do not. Similarly, they typically bypass costly activities such as research. In a further attempt to control costs, community colleges sometimes subscribe to management philosophies that they believe will help them run more efficiently and thus retain a cost leadership position.

A cost leadership strategy works for community colleges because most students who wish to attend a two-year institution are price sensitive. Community colleges also have been successful offering competitive entry-level general education courses. Many students and other stakeholders now perceive near equivalent quality between general education courses offered at a two-year institution versus a four-year institution. The main difference is that students pay a much lower tuition charge for general education courses offered at the community colleges, which essentially translates into a cost leadership advantage. In addition, as long as strong articulation agreements exist between different sectors of public higher education, the cost of moving from one institution to another in terms of lost credit hours is small.

DIFFERENTIATION

A second strategy is differentiation. In contrast to cost leadership, more than one successful differentiation strategy can exist in an industry. Differentiation has to do with discovering what is unique about a program or school that might be highly valued by students and potential employers of graduates (Wolverton & Penley, 2004). Uniqueness must also be perceived by those who will be buying the service (students, parents, federal government, etc.) the provider is offering.

The agricultural nature of public, land-grant universities differentiates them both physically and programmatically from other higher education institutions. The University of Idaho's campus incorporates a working farm replete with white wooden fences and barns. Iowa State operates a creamery, which produces Cyclone ice cream. Here, an agricultural product ties directly to the athletic team's name and the university's identity. Texas A&M provides still another example. The Aggie Code of Honor, which promotes ethics, dignity, and personal integrity, functions as a symbol to all Texas A&M students and alumni. The University of Idaho, Iowa State, and

Texas A&M all have unique characteristics that differentiate them from other institutions and thus help them attract students as well as potential employers of those students.

Rio Salado Community College in Phoenix, Arizona, is a prime example of a higher education institution that has purposefully and successfully employed a differentiation strategy. Its students tend to be working adults, not so different from those served by other community colleges. Its mission to deliver education opportunities to diverse populations throughout Maricopa County reads like most mission statements for public higher education institutions. But, from its onset in 1978, Rio Salado has been different. It operates out of an administrative building with thirty-three full-time faculty serving 60,000 students (26,000 FTE). It offers more than 450 courses and numerous associate and several baccalaureate and post baccalaureate degrees, particularly in teacher preparation, by employing more than 1,000 adjuncts and using online delivery systems in partnership with both public and for-profit colleges and universities. Courses start every two weeks. Administrators and staff who support this enterprise number well over 300. From its inception, the college has sought operational efficiencies through extensive use of Total Quality Management principles. Convenience, customization, expediency, and high quality are Rio Salado's hallmarks—a combination of attributes that differentiate it from competitors and make it a viable choice for students.

FOCUS

The third generic strategy is focus. Focus determines the competitive scope pursued by an organization within an industry. It requires that the organization establish a defensible niche within the larger marketplace. A college or university, even a prestigious one, cannot be all things to all people. By focusing, a college, university, or program targets a segment of potential students and tailors its strategies toward serving them to the exclusion of other students (Barney, 1997; Grant, 1998). It must establish a position within the marketplace that provides an identifiable image, which differs from those projected by other colleges (Wolverton & Penley, 2004). For example, the California Institute of Technology (CIT) targets highly capable students who are interested in engineering and science. CIT provides a premiere service because of the quality of its faculty and the extent of its resources, at an exceptionally high cost. In doing so, it sets itself apart from all but a very small handful of like-minded institutions.

There are two variants of a focus strategy: cost focus and differentiated focus. In both instances, the success of the strategy depends on establishing discernible differences between the target segment and other market segments in the industry. There must be either buyers with unusual needs, or the product and delivery systems that serve the target segment must differ from those of organizations serving other industry segments.

In some cases, a target market with unmet needs exists in a proximate location, but the buyers that constitute that market are too small for a given institution to establish a comprehensive operation in that market. Still, an institution may offer limited and focused programs that serve the needs of the market, at reduced prices. This strategy is well exemplified by the many public institutions around the country that serve a targeted segment of their state's population by establishing branch or extension campuses in remote parts of their states while remaining true to their "main" campuses. The University of New Mexico has its main campus in Albuquerque, New Mexico, but also has several satellite or remote campuses spread throughout the state. The affiliated campuses are located in small towns and they tend to be regional in scope; they have limited offerings but meet the needs of the populations in these locales. We now turn to two related strategies that can help institutions gain a competitive advantage: cost focus and differentiated focus.

Cost Focus

Unlike cost leadership, which is industry wide, an organization that depends on a cost focus strategy for its competitive edge establishes itself as a cost leader in one market segment. The information technology departments at Spokane Community College and Washington State University (WSU) serve similar geographic areas in the eastern part of the state. They offer the same Microsoft training and certification programs, which are designed for students who want to become network administrators, programmers, or system analysts. Spokane's tuition per credit hour is less that $75. In contrast, WSU's tuition is nearly $300 per credit hour. Each school has narrowed its focus to one particular market segment (people interested in careers in technology related-fields), but Spokane clearly has the cost advantage within the eastern Washington market.

Differentiated Focus

The differentiated focus strategy in higher education abounds. Differentiated focus does not require the organization to compete on price. In fact, if the focus is narrow and unique enough, the organization can charge higher prices. An organization that employs a differentiated focus strategy concentrates its efforts on meeting the specific needs of potential buyers in certain market segments. The use of this type of strategy implies that a segment is poorly served by existing suppliers. The perceived need to develop such a niche usually signals a real or perceived need to compete based on either services and products offered, geographic region served, or the audience targeted. Overall, establishing a niche requires that an organization expend concerted effort on a relatively small segment of its total potential audience (Barney, 1997; Grant, 1998; Porter, 1985).

In Atlanta, Georgia, two premiere state universities, Georgia Institute of Technology (Georgia Tech) and Georgia State (GSU) are headquartered within the same midtown business district, and both offer highly ranked MBA programs that to the uninformed observer might seem indistinguishable. Because they are publicly funded, using cost as a primary strategy is not an option. Yet, because each institution focuses its attention on decidedly different students and distinct curricular offerings, they successfully coexist in the same environment (Wolverton, 2006).

At Georgia Tech, in addition to targeting students interested in engineering and technology, the MBA program attracts only students prepared to matriculate through a 60-credit course of study full-time (Blum & Bennett, 2004). In comparison, GSU's Robinson College of Business caters to a working clientele by offering flexible, part-time programming, which meshes well with GSU's identity as a metropolitan university.

DePree (Georgia Tech's business college) builds programs across colleges (e.g., the masters in management and engineering and the master's in quantitative and computational finance) that align perfectly with the Institute's overall strategic direction of blending engineering and technology. In contrast, curricular decisions at Robinson (GSU) are not driven by one unifying theme but three: entrepreneurialism, e-commerce, and ethics. Each of these three areas is taught within the context of international business practices. Each specialization directly reflects the community that Robinson serves. GSU's business school capitalizes on and complements the city's business environment, which appeals to entrepreneurs and business startups. The school also responds to corporate concerns in banking and insurance firms headquartered in Atlanta about ethics and ethical behavior (McKillips with Mullen, 2004).

Combining Focus and Differentiation: Opportunities and Challenges

Both Georgia State and Georgia Tech successfully combine focus and differentiation. Because they limit the number of students they serve, one institution's success is not dependent on the other institution's failure. Each institution also possesses the resources to deliver the programs they offer. In contrast, Silver University's (pseudonym) creation of an executive doctoral program (also a differentiated focus strategy) demonstrates that organizations must anticipate and properly manage the byproducts of innovative action in their quest to gain a competitive edge.

SU is located in a rural state with one major city and two mid-sized cities. All three cities collectively house more than half of the state's population. SU is one of two major universities in the state; several regional universities are spread throughout the sparsely populated but large geographical landscape. An expansive community college system has developed over the years, which provides access to those in even the most remote corners of the state. The college of education at SU has a department of educational administration, which increasingly finds itself in competition with for-profit institutions, regional universities, and the other major university in the state. The department chair tracked a pattern of enrollment drops in the K–12 administration programs for years. The disturbing pattern prompted a number of conversations with faculty, with the department chair hoping to open the faculty up to potential and new modes of program delivery.

Despite its shrinking K–12 enrollments, the department is unique in that it is the only one in the state that provides a complete course of study in higher education administration. Some of the other institutions in the state provide related courses but do not offer the scope and depth of programmatic offerings found at SU, particularly in higher education. As a consequence, the department chair strategically decided to market the higher education programs to make up for the enrollment shortfalls in the K–12 program. The strategy was sound, but since SU is located in a remote part of the state, the increased enrollments in the higher education programs were not enough to make up for the consistent shortfalls in the K–12 programs. SU's educational leadership program decided to embark on a new strategy to further advance its higher education offerings. The department chair, along with two faculty members, pushed to establish an executive doctoral program, via distance education, to target future community college leaders.

Credentialism has been on the rise across all types of educational institutions, and community colleges are no different. Executive leaders in community colleges increasingly possess doctoral degrees, and those individuals without one find themselves at a disadvantage during the application or promotion process. For all of these reasons, and because the department was struggling with enrollment, the remaining faculty members became convinced that the executive doctoral program made sense. There were additional reasons why the new program was strategically sound as well. First, there are a number of community colleges around the state, serving both rural communities and the three population centers. Second, the large number of community colleges spread throughout the state made the distance education mode of delivery practical and desirable. Third, the focused differentiation of the program would allow for premium pricing. Finally, faculty did not feel they would have to abandon the traditional higher education curriculum since many of the courses that would comprise the proposed executive program would overlap nicely with existing courses.

Faculty networked and lobbied central administration for support and modest seed money to start the project. Porter's three generic strategy model was directly included in the presentations given to deans, provosts, and other administrators whose support was necessary to launch the initiative. Figure 4 is a revised artifact, which shows the three generic strategies and how faculty articulated the preferred strategies to central administration.

Faculty successfully convinced central administration that the proposed distance education doctoral program was aligned with institutional goals and could help brand the institution because there would be a statewide demand for it. The strategic success of securing commitment for SU's executive doctoral program for community college leaders was, however, somewhat tempered by the implementation of the initiative. The front end effort of developing a strategy, convincing administration of its merits, securing seed money, and marketing and advertising for the program had been so successful that the demand for the new offering was overwhelming. In fact, in the first year of operation, the program admitted more than sixty students in its inaugural class. The department chair, the dean, and central administration were very receptive to the executive doctoral program because their focus was more on enrollment and revenue than the details of implementation. But during the first year, several faculty members opposed admitting so many students, given the inevitable workloads that would accompany such an enrollment surge. The course delivery was only half the workload equation, since doctoral students require committee members who work with them on research projects. Indeed,

Industrywide	**Differentiation** (Distance delivery of doctoral program; new and unique, no other providers offering anything similar)	**Cost Leadership**
Particular segment	**Focus** (Community College Administrators; employees who wish to become administrators)	

Figure 4   SU's competitive advantage.

both teaching loads and doctoral student advising eventually increased. The strategy of launching the program exemplified the classic paradox: the administrative reason for the *why* of the initiative was compelling, but the *how* of implementation was troublesome once the time for action was at hand. Gilbert (2006) finds that the why and how of our individual decisions confront this same tension, so it is little surprise that strategic decisions at the organizational level follow the pattern.

The how of implementation eventually reached a breaking point. Faculty who helped craft the original strategy but were against admitting so many students and did not want to increase their teaching responsibilities eventually left. Several debates centered around balancing quality with quantity, but in the world of public institutions the scales sometimes shift to the latter rather than the former. In fairness, the executive doctoral program has made some modifications and adjustments since its inception more than five years ago. Most professors who now contribute to the program are dedicated to serving this particular market segment and prioritize teaching above research.

The case of SU's department of educational leadership demonstrates the power of a differentiated focus strategy. The executive doctoral program was well conceived precisely because it was placed within a strategic context that combined two generic strategies. The challenges, ironically, arose as a result of the success of the strategy. The department is now generating a comfortable cash flow because of enrollment demand, but the national visibility of faculty has somewhat diminished. SU demonstrates that strategy can help create a successful initiative, but it also illustrates the need to proactively anticipate the potential implementation challenges that may accompany even the most fool proof plan.

BARRIERS TO EFFECTIVE COMPETITIVE STRATEGY MAKING

All strategy making suffers pitfalls, and strategies designed to help capture a competitive advantage are no different. An organization might develop a strategy, but a change in the environment makes the strategy obsolete. Suppose a university expands its ability to offer courses in the heart of a business district. To compete with a local community college and manage its costs, the university rents storefront space rather than purchasing land and building a facility to house its classes. If the rent it pays increases, the college might have to raise tuition to cover the increased operating costs such that the community college's cost leadership becomes large enough to lure students away from the university's programs.

An organization may embark on a reasonable differentiation strategy but fail to monitor its potential competitors. Perhaps, for example, students choose to attend filmmaking courses at a private art institute regardless of tuition because the institute and the program itself are differentiated from offerings at the local community college and public university. If the university begins to offer a well-designed film program, it will be able to do so at a cost substantially lower than that of the art institute. If the cost differential is great and the programs indistinguishable, students, previously loyal to the art institute would choose to attend the local public university, all else equal. In this case, the art institute has lost an advantage that will be difficult if not impossible to regain.

Similar problems can arise with a focus strategy. If a university offers a highly specialized program, such as dental hygiene, it targets a small group of students. If the community college offers a similar program but charges considerably less (a cost leadership strategy), this targeted student population might move from the university to the community college. A community college might even target a subgroup (pediatric dental hygienists might be an example) within the university target population and draw students away by out-focusing the focuser.

Finally, systemic issues often disrupt the implementation of current strategy. New presidents commonly undertake new initiatives to signal their commitment to change. Colleges and departments may become disillusioned if the strategy drifts from a previously agreed upon direction. In addition, top-down strategy making and planning at universities and community colleges often have the guise of bottom up participation, but the process eventually becomes too centralized and slows market response time. The inability to capture a market because bureaucratic stumbling blocks get in the way can prove to be a disincentive to faculty who might otherwise see the advantage of offering a new program or targeting a particular group of students.

APPLICATION QUESTIONS TO DETERMINE COMPETITIVE DIRECTION

In today's academic arena, failing to compete is not an option. However, competitive strategy making is a complex enterprise, and even seasoned strategists make mistakes. But colleges and universities that systematically examine their competitive options and ask strategic questions establish adaptive capacities. Fostering a competitive spirit helps unleash and channel some of the abundant creativity housed in colleges and universities toward preserving the well-being of the organization. In the end, any college, university, department, or program that seeks to exercise its competitive advantage may better discern what form that advantage should take by asking itself questions associated with the three major competitive strategies.

Cost Leadership Questions

The five questions below offer a guide for thinking about whether a cost leadership strategy is appropriate for your organization. Short explanations and examples follow each question to provide a better sense of what lies behind the question. The more questions to which you can answer "yes," the more viable a cost leadership strategy is for your organization.

1. Do you have access to or contact with a broad range of potential students?
Some institutions are conveniently located in densely populated urban areas and have a captive audience. Others might service areas where a large 25–44 year-old population with retraining needs exists. Both of these situations signal potential cost leadership opportunities since it appears the institutions have access to or contact with a broad range of potential customers.

2. Are your potential students primarily concerned with price?
If you have access to a large potential student population and they are primarily concerned with price, then there is good reason to consider cost leadership strategies. Characteristics about your potential customer base can suggest whether they are price sensitive. Demographic information on measures of income and poverty might indicate that your target market is first and foremost concerned with price. Institutions located in regions with plentiful service jobs, but a dearth of higher paying, technology-related jobs may wish to seriously consider a cost leadership strategy. In such an environment, students are looking for bargain educational prices since their monetary payoff in the service industry is less than it would be in higher paying fields.

3. Will the number of students who buy your services be large enough that you can take advantage of economies of scale and compete on price?
A cost leadership strategy operates on the notion of quantity and volume. That is, since services are not offered at a premium price, there must be enough students who purchase your services to make up for the cost of providing it. Organizations that compete on quantity and volume typically realize economies of scale. These organizations use their facilities and resources to full capacity, such that the cost of educating or training addi-

tional students decreases. There is a point when enrolling one additional student will require additional investment in capacity. Organizations that effectively employ cost leadership strategies know where this tipping point is located because they understand their cost structure and manage their operations very efficiently.

4. Is your cost structure flexible enough such that you can cut costs quickly, if needed?

A flexible cost structure is one that has high variable costs as opposed to high fixed costs. High variable costs can be cut very quickly, in times of fiscal austerity. Community colleges typically have higher variable costs than do universities because they make use of a large pool of adjunct instructors. Conversely, universities that employ a high percentage of full-time, tenured professors have to pay yearly salaries despite the fiscal climate. Universities in this situation have limited options when they need to cut costs. If your variable costs are larger than those of your competitors, then you are likely to be more flexible in terms of making adjustments to your service offerings should demand change or vary.

5. What is the nature of your competition?

If you have answered "Yes" to the previous four questions, then a cost leadership strategy might be a very viable option for you. There is one remaining question to consider, however. Are there a number of institutions and providers who are already low-cost providers in your service area? If so, then you must be able to better manage your cost structure than your competition if you are to adopt an effective cost leadership strategy.

Differentiation Questions

The following three questions can help a unit begin to identify ways in which it can differentiate its programs and services.

1. Do you have a new or unique offering relative to other competitors in your market?

The MBA programs at Georgia Institute of Technology (Georgia Tech) and Georgia State (GSU) use differentiation strategies. Georgia Tech emphasizes MBA-level training for students interested in engineering and technology, while GSU's curriculum emphasizes entrepreneurialism, e-commerce, and ethics. Both institutions can survive and thrive, despite being in close proximity, precisely because differentiation allows them to sustain a market presence. Does your institution, college, department, or program have unique offerings or are you positioned in a unique way that differentiates you from other competitors? How, specifically?

2. **Are there opportunities to create a new or unique offering in your market because of an unfulfilled demand or a recent change in the environment?**

Changes within an environment can present opportunities for an institution to develop and create unique offerings that differentiate it from other providers. The aftermath of 9/11 created a new interest in homeland security and a renewed interest in the importance of educating students in areas related to world religions and languages. Colleges and programs that mobilized people and resources to offer degrees in homeland security or emphases in Arabic languages and/or religions did so to establish a competitive advantage. Is there an unmet demand in your market? Have environmental events given rise to new opportunities for your institution?

3. **Does some aspect of your institution (prestige, location, etc.) carry enough cache that brand recognition is high—or has the potential to be?**

Ivy League institutions have high brand recognition for a variety of reasons: they have a history very much connected with the birth and growth of our nation; they have star professors who are celebrities in the academic, business, and government worlds; and their research capabilities are second to none.

Most institutions do not have the automatic prestige and brand recognition that comes with being an Ivy League institution, but there are opportunities to build a brand based on current strengths. The University of Texas at Austin has a higher education program that has chosen to emphasize community college leadership preparation. The program has built a reputation for producing a disproportionate number of top-level decision makers in the community college world precisely because it strategically differentiated its higher education doctoral program long ago. The Massachusetts Institute of Technology is a university whose reputation for attracting and producing engineers and scientists differentiate it from the plethora of institutions located in the Boston area. Prestige can be built at an institution or program level. When people think about the higher education program at the University of Texas at Austin, they think about top community college leaders; when people think about MIT graduates, they think about engineers and scientists making ground-breaking discoveries. Are these stereotypes? Certainly. But it is these perceptions, at institution, college, or program levels that create the brand recognition that leads to competitiveness based on differentiation.

Focus Questions

Finally, the last four questions help 'focus' an organization's attention on market segment and other niche strategies.

1. Is there a particular segment (niche) of the market that is currently untapped?

Market segmentation is a well-established strategy, but its importance has been heightened over the last ten years with the combination of emerging technologies and increased competition. People who buy products and services from education and training providers now expect unprecedented levels of customization, from POD casts to synchronous and asynchronous course delivery.

Market segments exist along an almost infinite number of groupings. Groups with some common attribute can exist by age, gender, race and ethnicity, location, occupation, and industry, to name a few. Think about the individuals, groups, and organizations that buy your services. Can they be categorized along particular dimensions such as age or occupation?

2. If a niche exists, what services and programs are its members looking for?

Potential entrants and existing providers are constantly working on solutions to fill the needs of emerging market segments. The key to tapping into a niche is to identify a common need among a particular group of potential buyers that no other provider is currently fulfilling. In the previous example of SU, the institution correctly identified mid-level community colleges administrators as a niche for doctoral-level education. No institution in the state or region was meeting the needs of this particular group of potential students at the time.

Penn's (2007) attention to what he terms "microtrends" may be the key to identifying a niche in the market. Penn believes that the power of choice that is increasing across our world is such that it only takes 1% of the population to create a movement that can change the world (p. xiv). In the case of higher education, the proper identification of a small group of potential buyers with a common but unmet need can provide the focus a program needs to survive, thrive, and fulfill its mission.

3. Is price a primary concern to the niche on which you are focusing?

The first task in deciding upon an appropriate focus strategy requires the identification of a viable market segment. The next step is to identify the unmet needs that exist within this segment. Several needs might emerge, and decisions must be made about the importance placed on each need by a potential buyer group. If the predominant need is provision of the service at a bargain price—because the segment is price sensitive—then a cost focus strategy is appropriate.

4. Is the niche you are targeting more concerned with convenience, quality, or some service feature other than price?

A differentiated focus is appropriate for a market segment that values something other than price. Successful online graduate programs routinely charge a premium price to the mostly adult learner segment that they target because this niche prioritizes convenience and access to curriculum over price.

Formulating a competitive strategy is a complicated endeavor that is best optimized by tapping the innovative ideas of leaders and employees. Systematic analysis of pointed questions, like those listed above, can help an institution, college, department, or program reach a point of convergence about which competitive strategies hold the most promise for the future.

CHAPTER 7

VERTICAL AND HORIZONTAL INTEGRATION STRATEGIES

Private business has long used the idea of "integration" to achieve efficiencies, enhance coordination of activities, expand market share, or gain greater control of its products and services. Integration is a competitive strategy that takes two forms: vertical or horizontal. Table 8 summarizes these two integration strategies, which organizations might want to consider during the strategy-making process.

Vertical integration refers to an organization's ability to control or influence activities and processes that affect its inputs or outputs. Vertical integration is strategic when the organization proactively seeks such control. Horizontal integration occurs when the organization expands its offerings

TABLE 8

Integration Type	Description
Vertical	Organization seeks to control or influence inputs or outputs:
• Backward	• Control or influence inputs
• Forward	• Control or influence outputs
Horizontal	Organization seeks to grow:
• Expansion	• Expand existing services or products
• Diversification	• Add new or complementary products or services

Innovative Strategy Making in Higher Education, pages 91–106
Copyright © 2009 by Information Age Publishing
All rights of reproduction in any form reserved.

or grows by diversifying into new, additional, or related products or services. Colleges and universities already employ some vertical and horizontal integration strategies but often do so absent a systematic analysis to weigh the costs and benefits inherent in their choices.

VERTICAL INTEGRATION

The wine industry provides an illuminating example of vertical integration strategies and how such strategies fit within an innovative strategy-making arsenal of any successful organization. The production and sale of wine begins with soil preparation and ends with a customer purchasing a bottle of wine. Consider how the Robert Mondavi Winery approaches this process. Mondavi produces wines in California's Napa Valley. Like many wine companies, Mondavi grows its own grapes, ages the grapes, and then produces and bottles the wine. Mondavi does not own any retail stores to sell its wine.

Mondavi is "backward" integrated because it controls the main input to make wine—namely grapes. The founder (the late Robert Mondavi) believed the vineyard to be an important component of the winemaking process, and the winemaker's judgment on soil, spacing of plants, and general growing conditions of the grape remains critical to the production of a quality wine (Roberto, 2002). Mondavi's attention to the vineyards enables the winery to produce a higher quality product than, say, Julio and Gallo jugs of wine. In contrast, some wine producers do not own a single vineyard but instead buy their grapes.

Wine production constitutes the heart of any winemaking business, but once the wine is ready for consumption, Modavi engages in forward integration by bottling its wine instead of paying another company to do so. Finally, although the Mondavi Winery will sell wine directly to the customer, direct sales do not constitute Mondavi's primary product distribution channel. Mondavi does not own any grocery stores or national retail outlets. Instead, large retailers, grocers, and liquor stores carry and sell Mondavi wine. If Mondavi chose as a primary strategy to own retail outlets and sell its wine on a mass scale, it would be engaging in an additional forward integration strategy. The company does not do this because the business decisions required to own and run retail stores are significantly different from those required to produce wine. Mondavi's core competencies and strategic positions would be diluted if it pursued these activities.

Forward and backward integration strategies can be as important to colleges and universities as they are to private businesses such as Mondavi. Vertical integration strategies allow colleges and universities to view existing possibilities from a new perspective or embark on new activities that can

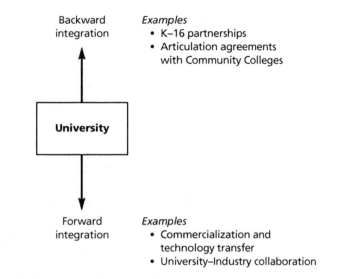

Figure 5   Vertical integration strategies.

enhance the production and delivery of education and research. Figure 5 presents various integration strategies for a public university. A similar figure could be constructed for a community college, a technical school, or any other institution of higher education. The examples for different types of institutions might vary, but the spirit of the concept remains the same.

BACKWARD INTEGRATION IN HIGHER EDUCATION

A university has many inputs: students, faculty, research, and money, to name a few. The extent to which a university influences, affects, controls, or directs these inputs is the extent to which the university is backward integrated. The backward integration strategies shown in Figure 5 are those that directly affect students.

The Strategy of K–16 Partnerships

Traditionally, large public universities simply reviewed the applications of prospective students and picked those they deemed most acceptable for undergraduate education. That model has changed a bit, partly because of legislative concern over student preparation for college and partly because of institutional recognition of its role in strengthening preparation. K–12 and higher education partnerships are now common across the United

States. These partnerships help align graduation requirements and admissions; reach out to underserved students; create opportunities for advanced students; alleviate remediation needs; and enhance teacher preparation, recruitment, and development (Mulchanow, 2005).

The Central York School District, located in central Pennsylvania, is involved in a K–16 Council with two local colleges to help produce feedback and identify factors to improve student math skills. As part of its plan to create a seamless transition from high school to college math, the Council analyzes indicators of student math performance (Mulchanow, 2005). This information is then used by the school district to redesign its math curricula. From the colleges' perspectives, this collaborative effort represents backward integration: they are working to improve their own inputs (students).

The federally funded Gaining Early Awareness and Readiness for Undergraduate (GEAR UP) program provides another example of backward integration in higher education. GEAR UP funds are provided for five years to states, and they require a partnership between higher education and K–12. The funds guarantee services to an entire cohort of students, beginning no later than seventh grade, and follow the cohort through high school. Some funds also finance college scholarships for low-income students (Gladieux, King, & Corrigan, 2005). From service to scholarships, GEAR UP affords university faculty and staff an opportunity to influence secondary students as they prepare for college. GEAR UP programs are, in practice, a backward integration strategy for willing colleges and universities, as they represent a way for institutions to influence and attract potential students.

Not all universities are involved in partnerships with K–12, and some that are involved are reluctant participants. By reframing a K–16 partnership as a backward integration strategy, the perception about the worth of investing effort in such an endeavor takes on new meaning. In every state, for example, there are a number of nonselective public universities. These universities compete for students with each other, with nonselective private institutions, with universities that are more selective, and with community colleges. A backward integration strategy of participating with K–12 in a partnership could be highly strategic for such a university. Universities involved in K–16 initiatives create relationships with K–12 school districts and their students. School districts might be seen as suppliers from this perspective. These suppliers provide an important input to the university, namely students. By establishing relationships with the supplier, the university better assures continued enrollment on its campus. At the same time, the partnership potentially improves the quality of students who enter the university.

Just as Mondavi Winery influences the quality and quantity of its input through backward integration by growing its own grapes, participation in a

K–16 partnership helps the nonselective university improve the quality and quantity of its input: quality by working with K–12 to improve student readiness; quantity by very likely increasing the number of students who will apply for admission because of the partnership. The cost is the time required to participate in the partnership, which can involve efforts to convince faculty and staff that the partnership is essential, valuable, and strategic. The benefits for the nonselective university clearly outweigh such costs.

Articulation as a Strategic Choice

Articulation agreements between community colleges and universities constitute another type of backward integration strategy, from the university perspective. When public resources become scarce, policy makers often look for efficiencies within their higher education systems. One perceived area of efficiency (from a policy maker standpoint) encourages students to start out at lower cost two-year institutions and subsequently move onto four-year institutions.

Highly regarded institutions within states are often reluctant participants in statewide roundtable meetings and dialogues that aim to strengthen articulation. Administrators complain that courses at the community college are not taught by Ph.D.s, and faculty indicates that they are too busy with research to work with the community colleges to standardize curriculum content. Top public institutions commonly pursue the state's top high school graduates and see little reason to shift any attention to community college transfer students. Those students who do attempt to transfer credits encounter many roadblocks. The credits typically transfer into the university, but then students have trouble getting the credits to count toward specific degree programs. Conversely, state and comprehensive universities tend to embrace articulation agreements more readily, working with their community college counterparts on concerns and issues regarding course curricula, course numbering, and student problems.

Institutions that embrace articulation agreements are, in effect, following a backward integration strategy, especially in light of demographic trends. In many states, universities face ongoing enrollment challenges as the 15- to 18-year-old population tapers off. State and comprehensive universities might still compete for high school prospects, but articulation provides an effective "hedge" strategy: if enrollment among high school students is slack, then incoming transfer students help make up the difference.

K–16 partnerships and GEAR UP programs provide a way for a university to influence potential students and develop relationships with schools and administrators who provide those students. Similarly, by offering options to community college transfer students, universities can influence potential students and develop relationships with community college faculty, staff, and administration. An important byproduct of such efforts is the goodwill that it develops with state policymakers.

FORWARD INTEGRATION IN HIGHER EDUCATION

Forward integration strategies employed by community colleges and universities vary depending on how they define their outputs. If job placement of graduates drives program growth, then college-to-workplace partnerships with local businesses can be considered a forward integration strategy. If a university views research as paramount to institutional reputation and visibility, then taking advantage of strategies that capitalize on university research outputs signals forward integration. For illustration purposes, we highlight forward integration strategies associated with research outputs (see Figure 5). Specifically, commercialization with respect to university research has generated considerable interest and debate in administrative, policy, and faculty circles, and as such is the focus of the next section.

Commercialization and Technology Transfer

Universities that conduct research have traditionally sought to publicly disseminate the knowledge that is generated as a result of that research. The sacred goals of public dissemination include the quest for new knowledge, recognition, and prestige. The dissemination of research produces recognition for the individual researcher or research team, and the university's reputation is enhanced as the research is conducted under its auspices. Researchers also expect that the knowledge they generate will stimulate additional research. Additional research can produce theoretical knowledge or knowledge that can be applied to a host of practical problems, inventions, or new ways of doing things. For example, theoretical research often is the impetus behind solving health problems or strengthening national defense. Industry interests have long played the role of building on university research (also known as industrial research and development) and producing creations that then can be sold in the marketplace for a profit. Geiger (2004, p. 194) states that traditionally the contribution of university science has been thought of as less significant economically than the intermediate contributions to stimulating and enhancing industrial research and development. Today, however, researchers and universities are very involved in the application and commercialization of their own research— their own output.

Before 1980, universities did not reap direct, substantial economic benefits from their own research. The Bayh-Dole Act of 1980 changed the motivation for research on many university campuses. It granted universities ownership of patents from federally funded research grants. Today, major institutions protect their intellectual property through patents, copyrights, and licensing. The Bayh-Dole Act creates an incentive for institutions to pursue research that (a) can be patented to produce economic benefit through royalty payments or (b) can be transferred to the market (technology transfer) for a profit, usually in conjunction with an industry partner who knows how to commercialize the findings. It might be argued that today's motive for research is more for the profit potential than knowledge creation and the public good.

Whatever the motive, universities generate profits through their intellectual property, and doing so reaches beyond the traditional function of simply producing research and disseminating the results. More than ever, universities can control the direction and use of the output (research) that they produce, which is by definition forward integration.

In the case of royalties, universities protect their intellectual property and then have the potential to receive royalties on that property. Large universities typically have technology licensing programs and offices that assist with obtaining patents, copyrights, and licensing rights. Monetarily, there is much at stake. Research universities, like the University of California at Berkeley and the University of Wisconsin, generate such significant revenues from patent royalties that they can be reinvested for other purposes to generate additional income (Blumenthal, Epstein, & Maxwell, 1986). Slaughter and Leslie (1997, p. 39) point out that, at least to some degree, these and other universities compete with for-profit corporations. Often, they also engage in university-industry collaborations whereby industry partners help bring university innovations to the marketplace.

University–Industry Collaboration

A typical university researcher (or team of researchers) that produces innovations and new technologies does not have the expertise to transfer the results and findings to the marketplace. University-industry collaborations provide a solution to this problem. This transfer of technology and innovation to the marketplace has as its main goal something that universities did not actively seek until the 1980s: profit.

Universities that seek collaborative work with industry for the purpose of transferring their research to the marketplace are embarking on a forward integration strategy. Geiger (2004, pp. 184–193) details several examples whereby universities explicitly create establishments that aim to develop application-based research or research that can be commercially transferred to the marketplace via collaboration with industry partners. The Georgia Tech Research Institute (GTRI) is the applied research arm of Georgia Tech. The GTRI is more concerned about generating practical applications for its clients than it is with enhancing its academic reputation or advancing theoretical knowledge. The GTRI offers its research services to for-profit clients as well as the Department of Defense. Researchers work with their clients to produce usable research, and the GTRI reaps monetary benefits from its associations and research productivity. Similarly, much of Pennsylvania State's research activity is best classified as Industry-Sponsored research, in which a specific for-profit organization funds research that is relevant to its operations. Research activities for both GTRI and Penn State are purposefully forward integrated.

Any organization that directs its own output in ways that vary significantly from how it traditionally behaved is following a strategy of forward integration. A strategy is no longer thought of as an integration strategy if it becomes conventional practice across similar organizations and no longer creates a competitive advantage. Integration strategies can also be controversial, as the traditions and values of higher education run deep. Although most major research universities are now involved in the commercialization of their own research, the controversy surrounding the appropriate role for faculty and university involvement in this endeavor remains. Forward integration strategies in higher education will continue to raise concerns because they create new ways of doing things that bump up against existing cultural norms. Even so, we might expect research universities to continue seeking forward integration strategies that have to do with research simply because the monetary draw is too great to ignore.

Costs and Benefits of Vertical Integration

Tradeoffs are inherent in any strategy, and different costs and benefits are associated with the various vertical integration strategies that an institution might implement. Different stakeholders have different perceptions of the costs and benefits associated with any particular strategy. The benefit of a strategy from the perspective of a university administrator might be seen as a cost by a student or policy maker.

The derivation of costs and benefits is not entirely objective, just as strategy making is not as scientific and mechanical as strategic planners would have us believe. Despite these challenges, an institution should go through the process of documenting the perceived costs and benefits associated with any potential or existing strategy. Disproportionate costs or benefits more easily surface through this process, helping leaders winnow through a multitude of strategic alternatives. Table 9 illustrates a cost and benefit analysis of the various vertical integration strategies discussed in the previous section.

The benefits of the backward integration listed in Table 9 suggest that these strategies help institutions establish a pipeline of quality students who seek enrollment. There are costs as well, such as faculty time and the generally low regard for service work on many university campuses. Articulation also requires additional effort for central administrators because they must work with department level administrators to accept community college transfer credits.

In terms of the forward integration strategies outlined in Table 9, the benefits of commercialization of research and university–industry collaboration are primarily monetary. A number of faculty researchers also derive fulfillment from seeing their research applied in a practical rather than theoretical manner. The costs associated with commercialization and partnerships are more conceptual and intangible: Do universities become too susceptible to private interests? Does the theoretical production of knowledge suffer? Questions such as these naturally arise when strategists conceive of new possibilities. The analysis of any integration strategy may be dubbed comprehensive to the degree that decision makers have examined the strategy with a cost-benefit lens and from various perspectives.

TABLE 9 Costs and Benefit Analysis of Various Vertical Integration Strategies from University Administration Perspective

Strategy	Vertical integration	Benefit	Cost
K–16 partnerships	Backward	Develops pipeline of students, creates enrollment demand; contributes to student preparation	Time investment of faculty, which is often perceived as having little reward; challenges in working with K–12
Articulation	Backward	Develops pipeline of students; creates enrollment demand	University faculty not usually in control of courses; difficult to get programs to accept credits
Commercialization and technology transfer	Forward	Creates additional revenue stream; faculty see immediate application	University begins to focus on dollars rather than knowledge generation
University–industry collaboration	Forward	Partnerships with organizations; industry helps in commercialization	Private sector has large input into research agenda; could sacrifice some public good

HORIZONAL INTEGRATION

Horizontal integration occurs when an organization expands its offerings or grows by diversifying into new products or services. Expansion builds upon prior knowledge, products, or services to create new offerings; diversification explores new markets and new offerings. Expansion and diversification are not necessarily mutually exclusive. An organization can offer a product or service that is related to but somewhat different from its existing products or services. Consider the company, General Mills. General Mills is in the cereal business. The cereal business is very mature, and competition is keen. Five or six major cereal companies compete for shelf space in supermarkets, and these competitors spend enormous amounts of money on advertising to win market share. General Mills vigorously competes for this market, but the company has expanded its product offerings beyond cereal to include snack bars. Snack bars are a natural expansion of the company's cereal offerings because many of the ingredients are already used in cereal production. At the same time, snack bars are a new product for General Mills, and one that can diversify the company's offerings and increase its profit potential if successful.

The behemoth corporations of the 1970s and early 1980s provide the best-known examples of diversification as a horizontal integration strategy. At that time, the dominant strategy for growth involved acquisition of new and varied businesses. General Electric was among the best-known organizations for expanding by diversification. Today, the company is still quite diversified, with its businesses ranging from light bulbs to appliances.

Horizontal integration represents a potential competitive strategy for colleges and universities. Horizontal integration allows colleges and universities to produce and deliver existing or expanded services to existing or emerging populations. As institutions take the pulse of students, businesses, and other constituents, they can determine the appetite for new programs and offerings. To illustrate this concept, we have chosen community colleges. Figure 6 suggests various community college horizontal integration strategies.

Expansion and Growth

Community colleges are widely perceived as institutions that embrace change and innovation. As traditional and adult students have flocked to higher education, it is often community colleges that provide them access. Community colleges provide low-cost options for students who are restricted by distance, time, or money. Community colleges have long offered a

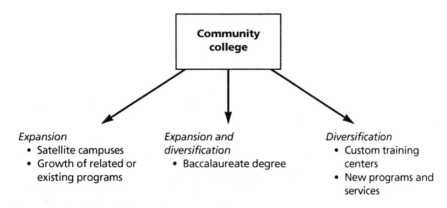

Figure 6 Horizontal integration strategies.

variety of programs and courses, but with growing demand many of these institutions are already operating at "full capacity." This means that courses are full, classrooms are fully utilized, and instructors already teach course overloads.

A community college might hire adjunct faculty to teach additional sections of a course given the overflow of enrollment. This is expansion. A purer form of expansion, and therefore horizontal integration, occurs when the increased demand for a given program is so consistent that the community college hires additional full-time faculty members to meet that demand. An even more dramatic form of expansion occurs when the community college establishes a satellite campus, with the primary purpose of offering similar courses as the main campus.

Community colleges also expand by offering new programs that may be related to existing programs. Technology enables new and innovative techniques to emerge within a profession, and this gives rise to new programs. Community colleges that choose to create new programs have the opportunity to train their students in these advanced techniques. The fields of radiology and nuclear medicine offer a good example. Community colleges offer associates degrees in both disciplines, but in the 1980s it was radiology that was prevalent. Advances in technology have made nuclear medicine an equally if not more popular degree program today. From the community college perspective, nuclear medicine is an expansion of its previous offerings. Although a student does not need a degree in radiology to enter into the nuclear medicine program, the programs are not mutually exclusive, from a faculty or administrative perspective. The community college must build relationships with clinics and hospitals that provide X-rays and nuclear scans so that students in either program can earn credits for internships, which in turn help with student placement after graduation. As such, there is some synergy between the programs because both are in the health field, both draw on the same organizations in which students are placed, and from a broad perspective, both enable a view inside the human body. In addition, there are some basic courses that students in both disciplines must take. If students are combined in the classroom for those courses, then the community college is creating synergy between the two programs in yet another way. Indeed, one sign of a horizontal integration strategy as expansion is that related offerings build off the existing internal infrastructure, the external credibility of the institution, and it's more established or traditional programs.

Diversification

A typical, comprehensive community college offers vocational programs, remedial education, general education courses, and community education programs. Customized training centers are one way community colleges diversify. Effective customized training centers can expand an institution's offerings, generate revenues, and build name recognition (branding) within the community. Many customized training centers that operate under the umbrella of a community college are essentially training companies that run like small businesses.

The operation and management of a customized training center are different from traditional vocational and general education offerings at the community college. For instance, the director of a customized training center must manage both revenues and expenses, whereas a department chair of a traditional program usually just manages costs. The training director must also market and advertise, create curriculum attractive to business clients, and work with full-time and contract trainers. In many respects, customized training should be thought of as a diversified service in the community college's portfolio of offerings. If the customized training center is meeting training needs, building the college's brand name within the community, and generating revenues, then the strategic decision would favor its continued operation.

Not all initiatives to diversify are successful. Many customized training centers have failed, for one reason or another. In one community college, the director in charge of the customized training program also had responsibility for community education. The director felt that the training program's impact did not justify its continuation and that it was too much of a diversion from the institution's focus on community education.

Expansion and Diversification

The strategies of expansion and diversification can coexist. It is possible that an institution of higher education embarks on a new initiative that builds on its existing expertise, yet the initiative takes the institution into unfamiliar territory. For example, community colleges that offer baccalaureate degrees are implementing a strategy of expansion and diversification.

Baccalaureate degrees at two-year institutions expand on the community college's current offerings. On the one hand, for example, most community colleges that award—or wish to award—baccalaureate degrees in nursing have long offered associate degrees in nursing. A strong faculty base already exists, and most programs are tightly allied with hospitals and clinics in their communities. On the other hand, community colleges that wish to offer baccalaureate degrees are diversifying, and with this diversification come new challenges. Issues of accreditation and curriculum are not immediately settled. There will be persistent questions about the minimum qualifications for faculty, and whether they should embark on research and not just focus on the traditional teaching function that is emphasized in community colleges.

The baccalaureate offering at community colleges is a strategic move. Community colleges currently offering the baccalaureate degree in select disciplines are successfully expanding and diversifying their existing portfolio of services. Not all attempts at expansion and diversification are beneficial. The board of regents in one state fired a community college president, largely over the attempt to initiate baccalaureate degrees at the institution. In this instance, political fallout as well as a lack of planning contributed to the unsuccessful attempt to offer four-year degrees at the community college, and it led to the president's dismissal.

Costs and Benefits of Horizontal Integration

Horizontal integration occurs in education and business, but it must be done with deliberation and care. The 1970s and 80s saw big business expanding by horizontal integration. Businesses such as General Electric became massive conglomerates, buying and managing very different businesses. General Electric is still a massive conglomerate, but it also has the resources to manage multiple (and often different) businesses. In higher education, horizontal integration, like vertical integration, has costs and benefits. Table 10 illustrates some potential costs and benefits of the various horizontal integration strategies discussed in the previous sections.

TABLE 10   Costs and Benefit Analysis of Horizontal Integration Strategies from Community College Administration Perspective

Strategy	Horizontal integration strategy	Benefit	Cost
Satellite campuses	Expansion	Increases the number of students served	Requires more resources
Growth in related or existing programs	Expansion	Increases the number of students served; keeps pace with business and industry needs	Requires more resources
Customized training centers	Diversification	Serves local business and industry needs	May be little synergy in managing different activities and programs
Baccalaureate program offerings	Expansion and diversification	Provides additional educational avenues for students, at a cheaper price and often at a more accessible location; may meet state and local needs in high priority areas	Resistance by universities; political fallout; mission creep; new accreditation, faculty requirements, etc.

The benefits of horizontal integration for the expansion strategies in Table 10 are largely about accessibility. As more students seek educational opportunities within the community college, central administrators contemplate the expansion of classes, programs, and even campuses. At the same time, community colleges must prepare a qualified workforce that meets business and industry needs. Private businesses that seek new locations often ask policy makers about the quantity and quality of the state's labor force, and community colleges must grow and expand to help provide that quality and quantity. The cost of all this is, of course, that growth requires additional resources. New facilities require initial investment, which student tuition alone cannot cover.

Diversification also has costs and benefits. Community colleges that diversify by housing a customized training center meet industry training needs and create name recognition and revenue for the college, if the center is successful. The benefits should always be weighed against the costs. In the case of customized training, costs are measured in terms of time and money. It is difficult to manage different businesses, since the services and customers are usually new to the institution. A community college that wants to grow through diversification must ensure that the administrator of the new venture has the interest, expertise, resources, and freedom to manage that business, otherwise the endeavor is doomed to failure. The same warnings apply to a community college that wants to combine expansion and diversification, as in the case of offering four-year degrees. The additional consideration for this particular strategy revolves around the political battles that are sure to ensue on the part of policy makers and university administrators. Political fallout is a potential cost, and one that the prescient administrator should anticipate.

The weight of benefits versus costs varies depending on the type of institution or program under consideration, the context of the strategic unit, and whether the strategy is vertical or horizontal integration. For example, the benefits of K–16 partnerships and formal articulation agreements might be palatable to a comprehensive university that faces declining enrollments. In contrast, a nationally recognized research university with high brand equity and name recognition might see little benefit in creating more enrollment demand via this backward integration strategy since it already rejects 70% of its applicants.

A team can begin the process of weighing the costs and benefits of vertical integration strategies by creating a dialogue around the following application questions.

VERTICAL INTEGRATION APPLICATION QUESTIONS

1. What are our inputs?
2. To what extent do we control the inputs before they enter our institution?
3. What advantages might there be in controlling a particular input before it enters our system?
4. What are our outputs?
5. To what extent do we control the outputs after they leave our institution?
6. What advantages might there be in controlling a particular output after it leaves our system?
7. Regarding the control of inputs or outputs: Are there individual costs to administrators, faculty, or staff that might overshadow the collective benefits to the institution?
8. Regarding the control of inputs or outputs: Are there individual benefits to administrators, faculty, or staff that might distort adequate consideration of costs?

The last two questions are quite important in that individuals often examine their own costs and benefits first. Individuals ask questions like: How will this affect my time? How much extra money do I stand to make?

Will I be able to obtain a course release? Strategists must be sensitive to such questions because the effectiveness of implementation depends on the motives of individual faculty, staff, and decision makers. If individual costs associated with the integration strategy exist, then implementation will suffer if the benefits are reaped solely at the institutional (collective) level. If there are individual benefits for faculty and staff, implementation is likely even though there may be intangible costs to the institution or the wider public good. Every strategy, including integration strategies, should be considered within the context of the organizational unit and the people who populate it. The final five questions below provide an avenue to discuss horizontal integration strategies.

HORIZONTAL INTEGRATION APPLICATION QUESTIONS

1. Do we possess adequate resources to expand?
2. Can current personnel effectively manage expansion or diversification?
3. Do we have, or can we recruit, the proper experts and professionals to manage our expansion or diversification?
4. Regarding expansion or diversification: Are there individual costs to administrators, faculty, or staff that might overshadow the collective benefits to the institution?
5. Regarding expansion or diversification: Are there individual benefits to administrators, faculty, or staff that might distort adequate consideration of costs?

CHAPTER 8

CANVASSING THE HIGHER EDUCATION LANDSCAPE

Several scholars (Mintzberg, Ahlstrand, & Lampel, 1998; Morgan, 2006) point out that early writings on organizations and strategy encourage the strategist to think of organization and environment as separate. The tenets of strategic planning encourage a reactionary sort of strategy, since institutions must look at opportunities and threats within the environment and align their own strengths and weaknesses, as an organization, around those parameters. Porter's five forces and the accompanying competitive strategies are also, in many ways, externally focused. Institutions assess competitors, consumers, and the overall environment and then formulate appropriate strategies.

In reality, institutions of higher education (IHEs) simultaneously affect and are affected by their environments. IHEs use existing technology, but they are also involved in its creation; IHEs target programs to fulfill the existing needs of business and industry, but faculty research and student innovation can generate new products and services that create markets or improve our standard of living.

The underlying theme of innovation is that colleges and universities do not have to limit strategy making to a process that at best only helps an institution keep pace with the top competitors in the field and at worst blunts any attempts at creating new services, products, or inventions. Institutions

Innovative Strategy Making in Higher Education, pages 107–124
Copyright © 2009 by Information Age Publishing
All rights of reproduction in any form reserved.

can move toward the future by using methods and techniques to help them create new markets. The perception of wild-idea brainstorming that breaks the barriers because people think outside the box with no limits is a fanciful notion that has little grounding in reality. Coyne, Clifford, and Dye (2007) insist that, ironically, breakthrough thinking and ideas can surface by asking a set of structured questions relevant to your business. According to Coyne et al., there are bad ideas and good ideas, and pursuing sensible, basic questions begins the breakthrough process.

Higher education strategists must also answer some basic questions to gain a sense of the "big picture" of their industry before breakthrough ideas are likely to surface. What are the characteristics of the higher education industry? Who are the relevant players or strategic groups? What are the things that colleges and universities do to stay in business? How do they survive? Why do people attend them?

Traditional strategy tools such as strategic planning and competitive strategy can help answer many of these questions, but part of innovative strategy making is combining and synthesizing information in creative ways. In this chapter, we primarily draw on an innovative tool called the strategy canvas (Kim & Mauborgne, 2005), to examine how new markets in higher education can and have been created. Strategy canvassing can be applied at the system, institution, or the program level. The strategy canvas is a creative yet systematic tool. This tool can help organizations generate new insights to open up new markets, yet its utilization is maximized by revisiting some classic strategy concepts. The idea of the strategic group (covered in Chapter 5), for example, is a prerequisite of sorts for understanding strategy canvassing. In fact, Kim and Mauborgne promote the insights that strategic group analysis provides, but they believe that examining relative positions within the same industry is informative only when one is interested in engaging in head-to-head competition or discerning what factors in one strategic group might be viable considerations for another. In a unique twist, Kim and Mauborgne (2005) advise strategists to look across strategic groups from different industries to see if new opportunities exist, something they refer to as Blue Ocean Creation (p. 79). By looking across strategic groups from different industries, organizations can derive new sources of innovation and competitiveness that are a combination of characteristics from those different industries. New sources of innovation and competition increase the reach and impact of any organization and can perhaps open up entirely new markets—an entire ocean.

THE STRATEGY CANVAS FOR THE HIGHER EDUCATION INDUSTRY

The strategy canvas concept is the culmination of years of research, consulting, and teaching. Kim and Mauborgnes' contribution is unique in that the strategy canvas as an analytical tool provides a way for organizations to look across industries rather than simply looking at competitors within their traditional industries. Another possibility in strategy canvassing is to include strategic groups into the analysis that traditionally have not been deemed part of the industry under examination. The strategist examines a combination of new and old competitive factors that leads to competitive advantage. Those factors that do not contribute to competitiveness do not figure in as prominently into the final strategy calculus.

The strategy canvas concepts can be applied to higher education not necessarily as a definitive answer to strategy making but as a useful tool that provides additional perspective throughout the strategy process. The strategy canvas is flexible enough to view traditional higher education competitors and explain why certain players are or were successful. A more sophisticated application of the tool to higher education can incorporate new competitive factors into the analysis by considering the operation and successes of nontraditional strategic groups. Part of the rationale for looking beyond the Postsecondary Industry is to incorporate nontraditional strategic groups that have previously been associated with industries outside of higher education. Training companies and corporate universities, for example, are part of the Global Postsecondary Education and Training Industry defined in Chapter 4 precisely for this reason. By incorporating these new organizational forms into an industry analysis of higher education, the strategist is able to examine a range of traditional and progressive competitive factors within a comprehensive analysis. Such an approach to strategy creates a new view of the industry and stimulates the kind of strategic thinking that presses leaders to think about how to create new markets, new products, and new services.

Throughout the rest of the chapter, we begin constructing a strategy canvas for higher education—but in incremental steps. First, we examine the traditional period of higher education up to1960, using the strategy canvas lens. This period was dominated by public and private four-year institutions. The analysis within the traditional higher education industry introduces the strategy canvas and its component parts to demonstrate its contribution to strategic analysis. A ctrategy canvas that only includes four-year institutions also provides the opportunity to gain facility with this powerful tool, so that subsequently it might be applied to increasingly sophisticated stages of analysis. In the second stage of analysis, we progress to the

Postsecondary Education era, which includes the 1990s. Here, community colleges and proprietary institutions enter the scene. We then examine the Global Postsecondary Education and Training Industry. This view incorporates new competitive factors into the strategy canvas because new organizational forms that were not previously thought of as part of the industry (such as training companies and for-profit institutions) are included in the analysis. We end the chapter by demonstrating how the strategy canvas can incorporate factors from outside the higher education industry by merging competitive factors for city government with universities.

The progression of the analysis in the chapter has the benefit of highlighting the evolution of higher education as an industry and the factors that lead us to a new definition of the industry. The suggested inclusion of new strategic groups into the analysis means that these same groups eventually become part of today's industry profile, but that too will evolve as the search for new strategic groups and new competitive factors moves forward. The chapter also demonstrates how to creatively use the strategy canvas in innovative ways to help institutions integrate successful ideas from outside the industry into their own operations.

Strategy Canvassing the Traditional Higher Education Era

The strategy canvas is a visual depiction that captures organizations, groups of organizations (strategic groups), or even entire industries within the context of factors that contribute to the production and delivery of goods, services, and benefits that customers receive from current market offerings (Kim & Mauborgne, 2005, p. 25). The factors that contribute to the production and delivery of goods, services, and benefits that customers receive are known as *competitive factors*. Strategic groups are plotted along these competitive factors. Each plot creates a line called the value curve, which is connected across all of the competitive factors. A value curve shows how an organization or strategic group within an industry competes or creates new markets along the different competitive factors.

The strategist is free to choose the competitive factors along which to plot the value curves. In fact, part of discovering what makes strategic groups or organizations viable is by analyzing different combinations of competitive factors. The selection of competitive factors is both a science and an art. Many competitive factors are prominent, well-documented attributes that obviously and clearly differentiate winning organizations. Other competitive factors are more intuitive and subtle, and it is only through thoughtful analysis that such factors emerge as essential elements of the strategy canvas.

The power and application of the strategy canvas to higher education strategy making are easily demonstrated by examining the traditional higher education industry. The traditional higher education industry consists primarily of four-year institutions, both public and private. Several factors that contributed to the past competitiveness and health of public and private four-year institutions are still in play today. To illustrate the construction of a strategy canvas for the traditional higher education industry, we pick three competitive factors along which private and public four-year universities are plotted: prestige, accessibility, and price. Other factors can provide additional insights, but these three factors create a simple view of the strategy canvas and therefore serve as an appropriate illustration and starting point.

Prestige is an attribute often affiliated with vibrant institutions, particularly when one looks at private institutions and their impressive histories. By the middle of the 20th Century, some private universities already had a three-hundred-year history. The roots of the prestigious Ivy League schools were inextricably linked to religious enclaves: Princeton by the Presbyterians, Brown by the Baptists, Columbia by the Anglicans, and, of course, Harvard by the Puritans. The premise upon which these institutions were founded has changed dramatically, but their established place in the higher education industry in no small part is indebted to their storied beginnings. The sectarian histories of the Ivy League universities still contribute to the aura and prestige of these mighty institutions, even though they are now nonsectarian in purpose and function. Prestige, to be sure, is an undeniable competitive factor within the private four-year sector.

Prestige is also important in public four-year institutions. Higher education has always had a "pecking" order of institutional prestige, which contributes to the so-called "arms race" among institutions. Regional universities consistently try to expand their offerings, hoping to attract research money and offer more graduate degrees. State universities continually seek a level of research status that will put them among the one hundred or so top institutions in the country. Every institution eagerly awaits U.S. World News Report's latest program and institutional rankings, with fourth-tier players gingerly explaining to constituents and the press why the rankings might not be completely valid—and top-tier programs and institutions explaining to everyone why they are. Clearly, prestige is as much a competitive factor for public four-year institutions as it is for private four-year institutions. Rightly or wrongly, institutional rankings by outside media sources often serve as a proxy of prestige.

There are other competitive factors within the traditional higher education industry as well. Accessibility has always been a cherished value embedded in the belief structure of higher education. Although public and private institutions may conceptualize the term in slightly different ways, the spirit of accessibility has many common threads. Stanford University believes that capable students who are qualified for admission should have access to its exclusive campus. In 2006, the university announced that eligible students with limited financial means would have access to Stanford because it would pay all tuition costs for those students.

Most public universities have an explicit goal of providing access to its state's citizens. A crowning achievement of public, four-year universities across the United States is that they have not only worked to provide pre-college programs and financial aid to create access, they have been successful in their results by many measures. If enrollment by income group is any indication of access, then public institutions are setting the standard. The College Board (2006) reports that enrollment in public four-year universities draws almost equally across different income levels.

Price (tuition) is yet another competitive factor in the traditional higher education industry. Price is related to accessibility, but it would be overly simplistic to say that they are the same. Stanford University's initiative to pay all tuition costs for qualified, low-income students creates access for those students, but tuition and pricing are used in other ways as well. It is well known that the "sticker-price" of tuition is often not what students really end up paying. Some students receive deep discounts, when institutional, state, and federal aid are factored into the equation. Institutions also offer scholarships to attract the best and the brightest students possible, effectively reducing price to attract these customers. Some commentators suggest that the elite, private universities serve two markets: the highly credentialed and the high income. Highly credentialed students receive admission on their merits and generally receive tuition discounts through scholarships; high income students receive admission because their parents are able to pay full price. Every business needs some customers who can pay the full price, and higher education institutions are no different in this regard.

Public universities also manage actual tuition charges in some of the same ways as their private counterparts, but not to the same degree. Price does serve as a differentiator for many public institutions, though, as some parents and students make their final admission decision based on price. If a high school graduate has been accepted to the University of Texas at Austin and Yale University, the student is assured of access. A potential factor for the student is the difference in the price of the two institutions, especially if the student does not qualify for any type of financial aid. The Yale education can be three times the price of the education at the University of Texas. For many families, this price differential is a competitive factor because it may well be the basis of the enrollment decision.

Figure 7 is a Strategy Canvas for the Traditional Higher Education Industry. The two value curves in Figure 7 are for public and private four-year

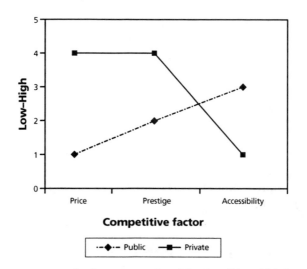

Figure 7 Strategy canvas for four-year universities (traditional higher education industry).

universities. The value curves are plotted along three competitive factors: Price, Prestige and Accessibility. Additional or different competitive factors could have been included in the strategy canvas, but these three factors are commonly understood as important differentiators within the industry. Plotting public and private four-year institutions along these three competitive factors also serves to illustrate the utility of the strategy canvas.

The strategy canvas in Figure 7 is a visual summary comparing the value curves of public versus private four-year institutions along three competitive factors. The value curve plots are simply estimates to compare one strategic group relative to the other. Thus, the numerical values on the vertical axis along which each strategic group is plotted on each factor are not exact, empirically derived points but relative positions that provide the strategist with a "big-picture" view of competitiveness along the factors.

The value curves in Figure 7 show that public and private institutions emphasize different competitive factors. For private four-year institutions, price and prestige are high, relative to public four-year institutions. The opposite is the case for accessibility. Competitive factors are often related, as is the case in Figure 7. The prestige of private institutions contributes to a perception of quality and exclusiveness, which allows such institutions to charge a higher price. The higher price, though, creates barriers to accessibility. Public institutions are more accessible because they are lower priced. Nationally, public four-year research universities enroll larger numbers of students than elite private four-year research universities. The costs of running any research university are significant, and public institutions must make up in volume (higher enrollments) what they cannot charge in price, which is one explanation for why approximately 80% of four-year enrollments are in public universities. Public institutions do not charge high prices for several reasons (e.g., they are subsidized by state governments), but they also do not possess the prestige of many private universities that enable higher prices.

Figure 7 is just an introduction to the strategy canvas. The higher education industry has changed over the years. New players now compete for students, and prospective students, parents, and policymakers no longer think of four-year research universities as the only option for education beyond high school. A more telling strategy canvas can help expand the view of who is competing and how.

Strategy Canvassing the Postsecondary Industry

The maturation of any industry is accompanied by different offerings and different players. The transformation of the traditional higher education industry into mass higher education and then postsecondary education gave rise to new organizational forms. Although two-year institutions have a long and respected history, it was their emergence in the 1960s and 70s that established them as major players in the industry. It is during this time that scholars such as Peterson and Dill (1997) generally describe the industry as mass higher education. As proprietary institutions came on the scene, largely enabled by federal legislation, education beyond high school became postsecondary education. Postsecondary education, therefore, includes traditional higher education, two-year institutions, and proprietary institutions.

The competitive factors of prestige, accessibility, and price continue to play a role in the postsecondary industry, but there are additional factors worthy of consideration. With the emergence of two-year and proprietary institutions, new characteristics of competitiveness began to surface. Some institutions began to focus their offerings. Rather than offering a vast menu of programs and courses, proprietary institutions often focus on a select number of fields. Proprietary institutions do not usually offer a full range of general education courses, and it would be uncommon to find such institutions offering majors, certificates, or concentrations in such fields as philosophy. The range of offerings among the many postsecondary players, then, is a competitive factor along which strategic groups differ.

Another characteristic that has changed over the years is *when* institutions offer courses. In the traditional higher education era, courses were mostly taught during the day. These business hour course offerings were well suited for full-time students who had few if any job or family responsibilities. As two-year and proprietary institutions came on the scene, they adapted the days and times of their offerings to the needs of their students. Evening and weekend courses are now common across all institutional types. Many courses no longer follow the traditional two-day or three-day a week, middle-of-the-day schedule. Even in traditional universities, students have a range of options. In many law schools across the country, interim courses are offered between semesters. The length and time of these interim courses provide great flexibility for students with different responsibilities and schedules. Some interim courses occur over an intense one week period, meeting every day in the latter part of the day, while other interim courses are spread out over a two-week period. It is probably accurate to say that student demand for course flexibility combined with institutional efforts to attract new students with varying schedules has led to more course offerings at times that are convenient for the students. Convenient course times represent another competitive factor in the postsecondary education industry.

The very nature of two-year and proprietary institutions also made it possible to obtain a terminal degree or certificate in a shorter length of time than the traditional four years required for a baccalaureate. The two-year time frame for an associate's degree became an attractive option for those wanting education beyond high school but who were not quite ready or did not want to enter into a four-year commitment at a university. Community colleges and proprietary institutions also offer additional degree and certificate options, giving students workplace skills in six-week or six-month time periods.

The education and training needs of a diverse population vary. Not everyone seeks a four-year degree offered only at certain institutions at specific times in a defined amount of time-to-completion. The different degree and certificate programs, with their different times to completion, have a place in the postsecondary industry and create a dynamic and competitive marketplace. Innovative providers, such as two-year and proprietary institutions, have changed the dynamics of the times courses are offered and the length of time it takes to complete a degree or certificate. This influence has spread to even traditional universities, which is a sure sign that time-to-completion is yet another competitive factor in the postsecondary industry.

Figure 8 is a strategy canvas for the postsecondary higher education industry. The figure incorporates some of the competitive factors from the traditional higher education industry (price and prestige but not accessibility) along with those just discussed. A strategy canvas must limit the number of competitive factors along which to plot the value curves, otherwise it becomes unnecessarily cumbersome and loses utility. One rationale for

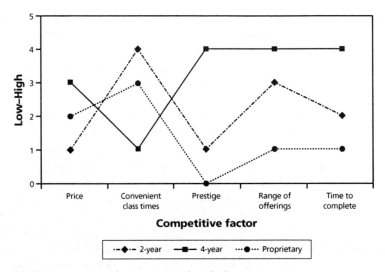

Figure 8   Strategy canvas for postsecondary industry.

keeping price and prestige in Figure 8 but excluding accessibility is that accessibility may be captured in other competitive factors. Accessibility might largely be a function of convenient class times, different times to completion, and price itself. For some, accessibility should be included in any strategy canvas, and, as previously mentioned, the strategist can create different strategy canvases with different combinations of competitive factors. That is the flexibility and utility of the strategy canvas as a strategic tool.

The strategy canvas in Figure 8 shows differences across the five competitive factors for all three strategic groups. The pattern of the value curves shows the most difference between four-year universities (public and private combined) and two-year and proprietary institutions. The closer the pattern and plots of any strategic groups, the more similar their offerings and the more directly they compete with each other. Whenever two or more strategic groups have equal or similar values on a competitive factor, then the competitive factor no longer provides an advantage to any of those groups. Customers are indifferent to either group, as far as that factor is concerned, and thus look to other attributes (competitive factors) to decide which service they wish to buy.

Two-year and proprietary institutions, according to the similar patterns in the value curves, compete more directly for students with each other than they do with four-year universities. This does not imply that four-year institutions do not compete with two-year and proprietary institutions for students, but it does suggest that among the three strategic groups shown in the figure, it is the four-year universities that are most differentiated from the others.

Normally, one thinks of a differentiated competitive factor as one that attracts customers, but a differentiated competitive factor could also drive them away. Convenient class time is a competitive factor in Figure 8, and universities are differentiated relative to two-year and proprietary institutions. Universities do not offer as many convenient class times. In this case, a low data point on the four-year university value curve provides an opportunity for other providers (two-year and proprietary) to attract students and increase market share. A high point on time-to-completion for four-year universities might be another factor that prompts potential students to consider two-year and proprietary institutions as education alternatives, as many students are eager to earn money rather than pay tuition bills.

Clearly, any given competitive factor can be viewed from multiple perspectives. Universities are higher priced and more rigid in terms of class times and time-to-completion; yet, the range of offerings and prestige associated with a university education are powerful draws for many students. Conversely, there exists a market of students for proprietary education and training. These students are more concerned about focused study and learning, convenience, and timeliness than they are about prestige.

The strategy canvas does not suggest that one strategy group's market for customers is completely different from another, nor does it claim that they are exactly the same. Different types of customers exist and different providers exist to attract these different customer segments. The strategy canvas is simply a tool to help view one group relative to another; to see if there is anything that can be gleaned from looking across related but perhaps different strategic groups; and to consider if, in fact, there are markets to be tapped by examining the competitive factors across a range of players.

It is fair to say that strategic groups influence one another. Most observers would not consider it an accident that programs and colleges across university campuses regularly offer courses at times and days that in the past would never have been part of the menu of choices. Community colleges have long been sensitive to student lifestyles and schedules and offered courses at both traditional and nontraditional times. Perhaps once these students experienced the flexibility of course times, there was a "spillover" effect that eventually made its way to universities. It might be that universities informally observed some benefits to such sensitization and the result is that programs at established and reputable research institutions today are more flexible than was true in the past. Whatever the case, the practices and actions of one strategic group influence, over time, the practices and actions of other strategic groups.

The next step in the strategy equation is to include strategy groups that, conventionally speaking, would not be deemed as part of the industry. It is possible that practices and actions used by such groups might stretch the boundaries of how we think about our own strategy and even our industry.

Discovering and proactively adopting or incorporating new competitive factors lies at the heart of strategy canvassing.

Strategy Canvassing Global Postsecondary Education and Training

The Global Postsecondary Education and Training industry includes new organizational entities that compete with the higher education institutions that previously or currently dominate the postsecondary industry scene. Individuals who would have previously chosen to attend a university or community college now have a range of choices as they seek education and training beyond high school. Emerging organizational forms present students with viable substitutes for education and training offered by postsecondary institutions. For-profit institutions are thriving and have introduced a whole new set of competitive factors into the industry. The instructor-industry tie is one such competitive factor. For-profit providers have indirectly (and sometimes not so indirectly) implied that university programs are populated with faculty who are theoreticians who do not possess the "real-world" experience of their instructors. Many for-profit providers that employ adjunct and part-time faculty require that these instructors concurrently work in the field in which they teach. The instructor-industry tie has struck a chord with scores of students who are seeking any and every insight and connection to segue into the world of work after they complete their schooling.

In an evolving industry, training companies form another strategic group, which can offer lessons across a range of competitive factors. Although many traditional academics might not view training companies as competitors, there is at least some overlap in activity between traditional providers and training companies. Organizations that characterize the training industry provide learning and knowledge and skill acquisition—all of which also fall within the domain of activity on traditional campuses.

Of course, training companies do differ from traditional institutions in many ways. Training companies and, to a large extent, for-profit providers, revolve their teachings around immediate job or task application. Immediate application of what one has learned is a competitive factor in the global postsecondary education and training industry because it has become a differentiator that resonates with students. Prominent characteristics of competitiveness, such as immediate application, should at least qualify for consideration in a strategy canvas of the relevant industry.

Just as training companies and for-profit providers have stressed immediate application, both have also mastered the art of marketing to potential students. Colleges and universities are increasingly using terms like "branding" and "marketing" to attract students and advertise their accomplishments. It is not uncommon to see billboards along freeways that advertise the benefits of attending a public university. Even with the increased attention that traditional institutions are giving to marketing, training and for-profit providers are second to none when it comes to this competitive factor. Training organizations and for-profit providers hire departments filled with business professionals with expertise in marketing and advertising. Both strategic groups reach potential students via email, flyers, and various other advertisements. Some of the marketing efforts contrast traditional university programs with what the for-profit provider offers. Training companies very often engage in mass mailing and advertising, knowing that only a small percentage of those receiving such information will enroll in their courses. Still, the mass mailing strategy is an explicit one, built into the process to introduce potential customers to the courses and their associated benefits.

Finally, in the global postsecondary education and training world, delivery options have expanded as technological advancement has enabled new possibilities. Universities and community colleges now have significant experience with distance education options, and discussions of Podcasts and online degrees are increasingly the subject of serious debate. Many institutions already offer these new delivery options. On the whole, however, it is probably safe to say that universities and community colleges are more deliberate and less likely to immediately embrace new delivery options on a mass scale compared to new entrants. In contrast, there are organizations in the for-profit arena that are entirely online. Online degree offerings exist at the undergraduate level all the way to the Ph.D. Questions of credibility and quality are continuously raised in reference to these organizations, but they exist, survive, and in some cases thrive.

Private companies and professional associations that offer training are also eager to experiment with new modes of delivery. The National Business Aviation Association is just one example of an organization that makes Podcasts of training sessions available to its membership. The thriving website lynda.com lists an entire menu of courses online and trains and educates thousands of people. Small business owners, entrepreneurs, and overscheduled professionals can receive training and education at their convenience, for as little as twenty-five dollars a month. They can access five minutes of training at a time or invest hours in one sitting, depending on their needs and their schedules. Webinars offer yet another growing vehicle for training and education, and seminar companies across the globe have embraced this internet-based delivery option as they expand their customer base.

As with the strategy canvas for the postsecondary industry, the global postsecondary education and training canvas incorporates a mixture of traditional and emergent competitive factors. Many of the factors that made four-year public and private universities or two-year and technical institutions competitive in the past are still applicable today. By the same token, there are new competitive factors that should be a part of the emerging industry view. The inclusion of these factors into the strategy canvas urges the strategist to "push the margins" and think about what makes different strategic groups within the industry successful. It might be that some of these competitive factors, or variants of them, are viable possibilities that can be incorporated into an organizational strategy for even the healthiest of the traditional providers. Figure 9 is a strategy canvas for the global postsecondary education and training industry.

Figure 9 plots the value curve for four strategic groups along six different competitive factors. Again, the need to provide a useful and telling strategy canvas means that some level of simplicity is necessary, so not every competitive factor from previous plots is included in the figure. The value curves in Figure 9 show some variation across the four strategic groups. According to the strategy canvas, four-year universities remain sufficiently differentiated from the other three groups along prestige and the range of their offerings. Even today, there is a certain mystic and deference given to the prestige associated with a four-year degree. The range of offerings and intellectual environment associated with universities continues to be a draw and is at least partly responsible for the longevity of these organizations.

For-profit institutions and training companies have similar patterns across a number of competitive factors, according to their value curves. Instructor-industry ties, immediate application, and marketing power are all factors that contribute to the success of both of these strategy groups.

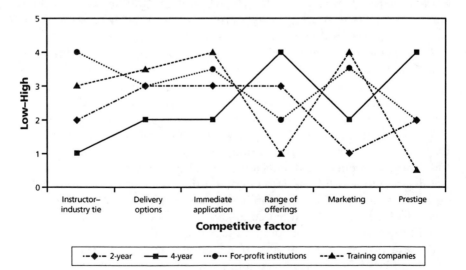

Figure 9   Strategy canvas for global postsecondary education and training.

For-profit institutions may market differently than training companies, and the focus of their courses and offerings might mean that the application of the teachings are in different fields and professions, but from a strategic standpoint, it is the characteristics of application and marketing that are of note.

The patterns in the value curves also indicate that two-year institutions will feel increasing competition from for-profits and training companies. In fact, many students attend community colleges to obtain certification or qualifications that are not associated with the traditional two-year associate's degree. Instructors in practitioner-based programs are usually skilled in their profession and have or have had industry ties. These programs are meant to provide immediate job skills to those who complete them. So, across several of the competitive factors shown in Figure 9, it is the two-year institutions that are least differentiated from one or more of the other strategic groups.

It is possible to construct complementary canvases using different combinations of competitive factors. The inclusion of accessibility and price would provide an alternative view and show the continued differentiated strengths of two-year institutions compared to other strategic groups in the global postsecondary education and training industry. A complementary canvas might include instructor-industry tie, time-to-completion, price, accessibility, and immediate application. The point of the strategic canvas remains the same: to creatively view the innovative factors that stimulate, expand, or create business across different strategic groups.

CROSS INDUSTRY CANVASSING

Throughout this chapter we have provided examples of canvassing within the traditional higher education industry and within an expanded higher education industry that includes nontraditional competition. In all instances, the focus has been on changes in the academic core offerings or delivery system as factors of competition.

Support services, such as those that deal with getting faculty, staff, and students to campus, from campus, and around campus, increasingly eat into campus budgets, particularly of those colleges and universities located in large metropolitan areas. Often, costs for land (if available) are high, congestion on and near the campus is problematic, and in some instances vehicle emissions exacerbate an already critical air quality problem.

Many college campuses resemble small cities. They operate post offices, medical clinics, book stores, retail shops and restaurants, law enforcement, office buildings, libraries, housing, and so forth. So, the logical industry for a cross-industry comparison might be large municipalities. For years, cities like Washington DC, Seattle, San Francisco, Atlanta, Chicago, and New York have dealt with traffic, parking, congestion, and automobile emissions. Their responses have included moving from surface lots to parking structures, encouraging ride sharing, developing mass transit systems, adding bicycle lanes to city streets, revitalizing downtown areas with increased housing options, and in a few cases embracing the use of cleaner burning fuels in public vehicles.

Colleges and universities have typically moved more slowly than progressive large cities to deal with these issues. The solutions higher education institutions employ tend to be predictable. When land is available and costs are reasonable, campuses simply build surface lots to handle parking. When campuses are landlocked and as enrollments grow, land once used for parking becomes building-sites for needed classrooms and laboratories. To compensate for the loss of parking, universities typically erect multistory parking structures to accommodate commuters, and they might encourage voluntary ride sharing or living on campus by building more dormitories. In the first instance, the congestion and air quality issues remain unchanged or even worsen because traffic is concentrated in a smaller area. In the second instance, commuters tend to keep different schedules and are disinclined to embrace the inconvenience of waiting for other riders to finish campus business. In the third, students who commute tend to continue to live off campus because they work, attend part-time, and are likely to have families.

In the 1970s, the University of California, Los Angeles's (UCLA) parking strategy profile matched that of most universities in the country. Figure 10

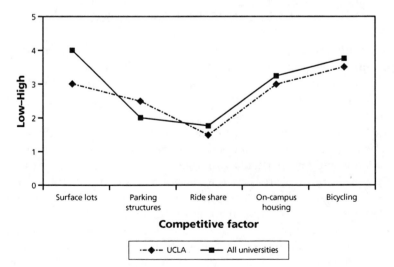

Figure 10   1970s: University transit and commuting.

shows a sample canvas of UCLA relative to all four-year institutions on various competitive factors, as they relate to issues of transit and commuting solutions.

In the 1980s, UCLA faced increasing pressure to find transit and commuting solutions for faculty, staff and students, especially in the midst of soaring land costs, increased congestion, and pervasive air quality problems in the Los Angeles area. All of these issues demanded that UCLA take more aggressive steps to handle transit and commuting problems while remaining sensitive to the environment. In response, the university instituted the UCLA Vanpool program (a combination of mass transit and ride sharing). Since its inception the program has eliminated more than 300 million passenger miles of travel to and from campus. Under the program, faculty, staff, and students who commute from more than 80 southern California communities are eligible to receive subsidies toward the cost of commuting as passengers in one of 150 UCLA-owned commuter vans.

Sustainable transportation related to smog reduction has received added attention from the campus community in its attempts at resource stewardship, environmental protection, and energy conservation. To this end, UCLA works with municipal bus companies to provide transit options through the use of discount passes—BruinGo and GoMetro. More than 23,000 staff, faculty, and students take advantage of these programs. The university also partners with Flexcar to provide members with on-demand access to a fleet of low emission vehicles located on campus. Its 112 campus shuttle buses run on natural gas; it increased the supply of on-campus housing to reduce commuting, promotes shared riding, and put in place a bicycle master plan, which has resulted in a 50% ridership increase.

Although strategy canvassing was not a technique used in the 1980s, the tact that UCLA took to confront its parking issues helps illustrate the power of strategy canvassing. Efforts to come to grips with and solve its parking and pollution problems and thus control operation costs in retrospect provide an excellent example of how college and universities can use strategy canvassing to uncover viable strategies by creatively drawing on effective competitive factors from other industries.

In Figure 11, we use the traditional university profile (a profile that remains unchanged, for the most part, since the 1970s) for purposes of illustration. We overlay it with UCLA's post 1980s profile and a hypothetical profile of large cities. The resulting picture points immediately to the similarities between UCLA's profile and that of big cities, and it draws attention to the decidedly different route UCLA took from the more common university approach to parking and transportation.

UCLA's strategies developed over time, but the university surely took lessons from innovative cities across the country and applied them to its situation. A strategy canvas would have provided a systematic and more timely

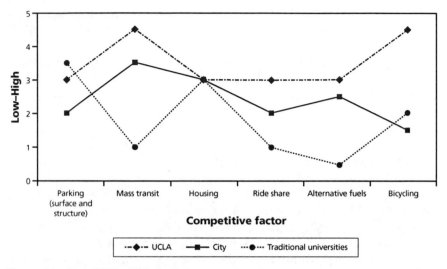

Figure 11   Post-1980s: Transit and commuting.

way to gain an overall strategy picture and point to innovative approaches to the problems they faced.

THE ADVANTAGES OF STRATEGY CANVASSING

The strategy canvas as a tool provides the opportunity to create multiple views of an industry across multiple competitive factors. The process of creating multiple strategy canvases with different combinations of competitive factors across the industry is a systematic exercise that can help decision makers gain insight into the characteristics that drive or can drive success within that industry. The technique also provides flexibility in that those who strive for innovation and new ideas are free to include competitive factors from other industries that might be applicable to higher education's core or support businesses. Such idea prospecting is another way to imagine the future and possibly create new markets by integrating the strengths of different industries into one's own strategic thinking.

The strategy canvas is a mechanism that affords higher education organizations the opportunity to think about a fundamental strategic question: what new or little considered factors might allow us to differentiate ourselves, better serve existing customers, attract new ones, and expand the good work that we do? It, as much as any strategy tool to date, provides a logical and systematic way to help uncover the answers to these questions.

CHAPTER 9

THE STRATEGY AND INNOVATION NEXUS

Contrary to popular belief, most innovations result from a conscious, purposeful search for opportunity. Strategy tools, from planning to canvassing, provide systematic means by which to find and exploit opportunity through innovation. Chapters 2–8 formally present various strategy tools that are at the strategist's disposal. Innovative leaders use one tool, parts of tools, or a combination of tools to create new products or services.

Strategists may also create new techniques and methods and then use them in combination with established strategies. Whatever the means to effective strategy, innovation is at the core—whether that strategy seeks to solidify one's competitive position or entrepreneurially create new market space.

Drucker (2002) identified seven sources of innovation, four internal to the organization or industry and three that exist in the external environment. An adaptation of Drucker's framework is shown in Table 11. The relationship between the sources of innovation and strategy tools is that any tool (or combination of tools), existing or new, can be used to generate innovative services or products.

Drucker's sources of innovation are not without debate in the sense that there is reasonable question as to whether certain sources truly lead to innovation or efficiency improvement. It is the organizational response to the

Innovative Strategy Making in Higher Education, pages 125–137
Copyright © 2009 by Information Age Publishing
All rights of reproduction in any form reserved.

TABLE 11   Adaptation of Drucker's Sources of Innovation

Internal to the Organization/Industry	External in the Environment
Unexpected Occurrences	Demographic Changes
Incongruities	Changes in Perception
Process Needs	New Knowledge
Industry and Market Changes	

potential source of innovation and the tools that are used to respond to it that determine whether actual innovation takes place.

The first source of innovation internal to the organization is unexpected occurrences, which are unplanned opportunities. Those institutions that are able to proactively capitalize on unplanned opportunities through, say, expanding their vision and establishing new goals, put themselves in a strategic position to expand existing market offerings, serve new markets, or create new offerings. When the federal government began closing military bases, the state of California took over Fort Ord as the site for California State University, Monterey Bay. The purchase of this site allowed the California State System to expand horizontally but also to establish infrastructure to serve new markets and potentially offer new educational services given the uniqueness of the facilities and their locations.

Incongruities are also a potential source of innovation, often manifesting themselves in economic terms. When supply and demand are not in equilibrium, an incongruity exists and presents an opportunity for those who recognize it and are willing to act on it. For-profit organizations, such as art institutes and schools of fashion, design, culinary arts, and media, charge premium prices for two-year associate degrees. Their ability to do so points to an unmet need, which is an indication of an incongruity in the marketplace. These organizations capitalize on this incongruity by building programs that appeal to differentiated niches, which are willing to pay higher tuition for focused and convenient programs. Incongruities can be filled by existing market providers or new entrants who quickly seize the opportunity.

Like unexpected occurrences and incongruities, market and industry changes often present an opportunity for significant changes in how colleges and universities do business. One of the most influential market changes in higher education in the past ten years emanates from changes in program and course delivery. Some colleges have greatly expanded their student enrollments by 'going' online and capturing market share from competitors who are reluctant to engage in such endeavors.

Drucker also lists process needs as a potential internal source of innovation. Although the process used to deliver education services might not directly present significant opportunity for innovation in higher education, ancillary processes that keep a college or university running smoothly often do. Taking advantage of such opportunities frees up monies that can then be used to further the education of students. Process needs usually stem from the necessity to control costs and use resources wisely in ways that improve service and, in some instances, reduce potential ill effects to the environment. Streamlining the book ordering process and course scheduling through computerized systems that retain records from year-to-year save faculty and administrators time. Recycling wastewater to use on landscaping is another example. Such process improvements usually bring about efficiencies that sometimes, as we discuss later in this chapter, also lead to innovation in educational programs and curriculum.

All three sources of innovation listed as external in Table 11 hold the potential for colleges and universities to compete more effectively or create new services and offerings in the entrepreneurial sense. Demographics factor into the strategy calculus in virtually all of the tools we have discussed in this book, from strategic planning and PEST to industry analysis and strategy canvassing. Changes in demographics, by age, race/ethnicity, and gender are highly predictable because public reports and statistics are available on high school graduates, the growth in the 25–44 year-old population, and so on. Each of these trends offers opportunities for existing and emerging education-related organizations.

Some aspects of demographics are not easily predicted. Changes in perceptions of any given demographic group are more difficult to discern than is the growth in numbers of a particular age group. Perceptions have to do with changes in preferences, needs, wants, expectations, political feelings, and social mores, all of which evolve over time.

Perceptions about the credibility and viability of online education have shifted from a deficit model to an accepted mode of education. These changes in perception have certainly impacted higher education as an industry, both in the for-profit and nonprofit domain. Online colleges and universities are many times equated with for-profit or private providers, but these perceptual changes have not escaped public officials. Western Governors University, the online university collaboration founded by 19 governors of western states, is a prime example of how the acceptance of online education has generated new providers, new degree programs, and, of course, new delivery mechanisms.

Finally, Drucker cites new knowledge as a source of innovation. New knowledge is the foundation upon which higher education institutions rest. New knowledge can emerge in teaching or research. It stimulates everything from course delivery systems that drive changing perceptions to creative organizational designs that enable institutions to perform their functions or provide access more effectively. There is no question that new knowledge offers the potential for innovation, but it is organizational action that determines whether that potential is transformed into a strategy that produces real innovation.

COMPETITIVENESS VERSUS ENTREPRENEURIALISM

Whatever the sources and characteristics of innovation, the results associated with it manifest themselves in one of two ways: enhanced competitiveness or entrepreneurial creation. Competitiveness is about learning to work within an established environment. Being entrepreneurial is about creating new market space. A competitive organization adapts to or capitalizes on the parameters set by the environment so that the organization can establish a competitive edge and/or expand the market. An entrepreneurial organization creates a new environment and establishes new market space in which to operate.

Using innovation to enhance competitiveness means that organizations work with long, future-oriented time lines as they attempt to maintain clear visions of what they want to accomplish in the face of anticipated changes within their existing environments. The exercise draws organizational members together as they move in an agreed upon direction that is defined by the vision. Competitive organizations can expend available monies more wisely and stand to profit more if they pay attention to those places their competitors overlook (Galbraith, Lawler, & Associates, 1993) or if they refine or evolve their product or service offerings. The vision and the direction do not revolutionize the product or service offerings of the organization. Instead, the organization increases its hold on existing markets, finds a new niche (by segmenting the market) for its current product or service, or simply wins the competition for customers among a given group of competitors. The most competitive organizations work to shape a future that clearly distinguishes their efforts from those of others that also function within a given environment (Porter, 1985; Wolverton & Penley, 2004).

In contrast, innovative entrepreneurialism refers to the creation of a market in which there are no competitors. Small, entrepreneurial organizations, whether in business or education, usually gain viability precisely because they offer something unique and different. Market advantages accrued by entrepreneurial organizations are usually short-lived and unsustainable. Once entrepreneurial organizations reach a certain success threshold, they undergo changes that, ironically, make it difficult to hold onto their advantage. First, out of necessity, the organization changes its structure to cope with its success. It becomes larger, which leads to a need for more rules and a bureaucratic structure to accommodate the growth and deal with the complexities that result from hiring more people, doing more advertising, and running a larger business. In doing so, it loses some of the agility it needs to deal with the competition that success invariably breeds. Second, other organizations begin to see that if they can replicate (perhaps at a lower price) or slightly modify the entrepreneur's product or service they might be able to capture market share. It is the inevitable draw of a new market that attracts competitors (and spurs competitive innovation), who are now able to quickly learn from all of the lessons that the entrepreneurial organization so painfully experienced on its path to success. In other words, the experience curve takes less time to travel for competitors who come after the entrepreneurial organization that blazed the original trail.

COMPETITIVE AND ENTREPRENEURIAL INNOVATION IN THE BUSINESS ARENA

In the business arena, a company can be at the helm of entrepreneurial innovation in one instance and using innovation to obtain a competitive edge in another. In the history of the computer, IBM's entrepreneurial spirit led to a new market for mainframe computers for big business and government. This same IBM failed to see a new market space that Apple saw in desk-top computers for small business and the general public. Apple soon lost its entrepreneurial advantage to the competitive hand of IBM, Gateway, Tandy, Dell, HP, and a host of others, who sensed that they could make money by producing similar products. Apple regained its entrepreneurial status when it created another new product and, more important, a new market space in which to operate with the inception of the iPod and all its subsequent variations. Currently, Apple dominates this new market space, but Microsoft's Zunes or other products will certainly make inroads and possibly erode the advantage Apple originally gained through entrepreneurial innovation.

Compared to Apple's entrepreneurialism, Microsoft's innovative advantages are distinctly competitive in nature. Historically, the company has created variations of products already in the marketplace. Microsoft Office grew out of the operating system, DOS; Microsoft Word stems directly from WordPerfect; Internet Explorer from Netscape; Access from D-Base (an IBM product), and Excel from Lotus. Observers and historians often argue that the superiority of an original product may be of little consequence when a formidable competitor enters the ring. Indeed, Microsoft's current dominance is largely attributable to its marketing power as it expands its influence in the existing marketplace of software products.

COMPETITIVE ACTION IN HIGHER EDUCATION

Competitiveness and entrepreneurialism apply to higher education as well as business. Public community colleges and universities often find themselves competing with each other and with other public agencies for state funding and resources, particularly in times of economic austerity. Competition is also keen for students, as institutions jockey to attract new students through marketing efforts, developing infrastructure, or creating new programs and curriculum. In such an environment, institutions must look for innovative approaches to competition if they are to survive.

In the remainder of this chapter we profile examples of successful competitive and entrepreneurial strategies executed by colleges and universities. The colleges and universities that we feature foster cultures where change is expected and accepted, and prudent risk taking that results in proactive change is preferable to alternatives that are dictated by entities outside the institution. Like IBM and Apple, some of these institutions saw new possibilities; others discovered new combinations of people, strategies, and other resources in much the same way as did Microsoft. All embarked on the innovation road with a clear set of goals.

Going Green as a Competitive Innovation

In a state where higher education operating budgets suffer yearly reductions, Lane Community College in Eugene, Oregon, has proactively sought ways to cut costs and at the same time "green" its campus. When organizations are faced with resource cuts, many turn to process improvement as a way to increase efficiencies and thus save costs. Lane was no different but added a slightly different twist by examining how it might reduce its utility costs and simultaneously engage in responsible stewardship of its environment. The college has saved thousands of dollars by revamping its heating, ventilation, and lighting systems. It conserves water by using automatic flush toilets. Its kitchens compose food waste. Clothing and surplus property exchanges keep used and unwanted articles out of the trash. As a result, the school's recycling/reuse rate in 2006 was 61%. It reduced the use of pesticides from 650 pounds to less than 10 and has plans for upgrading its maintenance fleet to include only hybrid and electric vehicles. Wind power provides 10% of its electricity, a percentage that will increase in the future.

What makes Lane unique is that the institution leverages its efforts toward process improvement to also improve the competitiveness of its certificate programs. Lane incorporates its own practices and experience in conservation into a two-year energy management program and a chemistry program. The integration of greening and conservation into the program areas differentiates them and provides real world opportunities for students, thus increasing the visibility and competitiveness of the programs. Student volunteers can work with campus staff on the various environmentally friendly efforts occurring on campus, thus bearing witness to the teachings found in their programs.

Cape Cod Community College in Massachusetts, like Lane, also translates its own greening efforts into a competitive advantage by integrating those efforts into its core offerings (academic programs). For more than ten years, Cape Cod has focused the community's attention and the education of its students on the importance of environmental sustainability. Its curricula, facilities management, and widespread influence attest to its success. The college offers several environment and sustainability-related degrees that are enhanced by its own practices, which include using passive solar energy, smart lighting, grey-water recovery, permeable paving, recycled construction products in its new buildings, and reduced water consumption. In addition, Cape Cod continually works with several local and state agencies, including the Massachusetts EPA, Cape and Islands Renewable Collaborative, and the Farmer's Market, which links local growers with local restaurants as an economic development initiative, to promote its and the region's sustainability efforts. Clearly, the connections the college makes with outside constituents is yet another competitive differentiator, enabled by its focus on environmental sustainability.

INNOVATION THROUGH ENTREPRENEURIALISM

A common theme across studies on creativity and innovation suggests that something new can arise by combining previously independent parts into a new whole. The new creation is an innovative synthesis that opens up new markets. Ice cream and soda were not co-created, but the creative synthesis of the two has given joy to millions in the form of the now famous delicacy we call the float.

When colleges and universities find new resources or employ existing ones to create new possibilities in teaching, research, or service, they are creating new space and new markets in which to operate. In higher education, entrepreneurialism occurs in programs and entire institutions. In the following examples, Evergreen State College derives its innovative spirit from a mission that directs it to unconventionally fulfill its social contract with the citizens of the state of Washington. Colorado State University engages in entrepreneurial behaviors that, in part, are economically driven but also address a mandate to be socially responsible.

Evergreen State College

Interdisciplinary studies in higher education are sometimes given great rhetorical deference, but few institutions actually focus on and reward initiatives that draw on the interdisciplinary power that resides on their campuses. Evergreen State College in Olympia, Washington, is different.

Evergreen opened its doors in the early 1970s as a nontraditional experimental institution. Its faculty conducts narrative evaluations of students' work instead of grading it. Students enroll in team-taught, year-long seminars, called Coordinated Studies Programs, which bring together seemingly divergent disciplines and areas of study. For example, combining music, cultural studies, leadership, and sailing affords students the opportunity to explore the individual's relation to self, society, leadership, and the creative process. Biology, the history of technology, American studies, and the philosophy of science help students examine the nature of biological evolution and patterns of technological, social, and cultural change over three centuries of American history. Knowing Nature draws on faculty from classical studies, philosophy, physics, and applied mathematics. Money, Molecules, and Meds is taught by faculty who specialize in management, chemistry, statistics, and pharmacology. The course explores the economic, ethical, and scientific impact of the pharmaceutical industry on global society. Its master's of environmental studies perhaps best captures the interdisciplinary nature of Evergreen's programs. This program integrates biological, physical, and social sciences with public policy and politics. The program's goal is to provide "quality professional preparation for people working at the intersection between environmental science and societal policymaking in the public, private, and nonprofit sectors."

In its relatively short existence, Evergreen has established itself as a national leader in the development of interdisciplinary learning communities and environmentally conscious academic programming. Evergreen's approach is predicated on its entrepreneurial creations, which can be aptly thought of as an effective fusion of disciplines that create a unique student (and, no doubt faculty) experience.

Colorado State University

While Evergreen serves as a shining example of entrepreneurial innovation in teaching and program development, Colorado State University (CSU) offers an equally entrepreneurial counterpart in the area of research and technology transfer. CSU is a land grant, research-extensive university. Like many research institutions, CSU struggled to transfer its research findings to the marketplace in a timely, affordable, and profitable manner.

In the past, CSU researchers typically took ideas to the CSU Research Foundation. The Foundation evaluated each idea for marketability, potential for licensing, opportunity for growth, and effort it would take to develop. Promising ideas moved toward commercialization through co-development with the private sector, licensing to a private company, or the efforts of a start-up company.

The university has now created what are called Superclusters. Superclusters are interdisciplinary alliances that simultaneously allow business experts to gauge marketability and scientists to do the research. In effect, Superclusters speed up the process of research and development and commercialization by applying business practices to the university setting. Each Supercluster is organized in a specific scientific area and has a chief science officer who oversees research activities and a chief operating officer who focuses on forging business alliances and developing new opportunities for the results of the research (this person is typically from business). A technology transfer specialist seeks opportunities for patents, licenses, and startups, as well as equity investors.

In designing these clusters, CSU chose areas where it holds preeminence in research and where a great global challenge exists. The notion is to play a central role in creating solutions to global health, environment, and energy issues. The university systematically looks for overlap between expertise and global need. This global-need parameter provides focus for university wide research efforts.

CSU's first Supercluster, MicroRx, (operational in early 2007 after three years of planning) deals with infectious diseases. MicroRx involves the work of a wide group of experts—clinical scientists, pathologists, microbiologists, business ethicists, and political scientists, all working to advance medicine for the public good. Its primary goal is to "expeditiously commercialize intellectual property for society's health by developing medical interventions that save and improve lives faster and with more precision to fill gaps in current medicine." Future Superclusters will specialize in cancer, clean energy, environmental science, and agriculture research. Any of these Superclusters could involve public policy specialists, social scientists, linguists, engineers, economists, and manufacturing professionals, working along side research and business specialists.

This new, more entrepreneurial approach to technology transfer carries several benefits. First, researchers can focus on their areas of expertise and not worry about transfer issues. Second, businesses can work more easily with CSU to move research from the academy into the marketplace. Third, Superclusters foster more collaboration and less territorialism. The university suspects that, in the long run, Superclusters will serve as magnets for scholars in other disciplines. In addition, government, philanthropic, and corporate entities will benefit from CSU's research. Finally, CSU believes that it will be able to take advantage of more transfer opportunities by focusing on specific areas where it already excels and a critical need exists. CSU estimates that Superclusters will allow it to more than double the number of innovations and startups resulting from all scientific findings in the next five years.

WHAT IS THE INNOVATION FORMULA?

In its history, IBM has gone through periods of innovation fueled by entrepreneurialism. In other periods, the company survived and thrived because its competitive fire allowed it to distance itself from other players in the same market. Higher education institutions, like companies, can find themselves moving from entrepreneurial creation to competitive action. The higher education examples in this chapter are neatly categorized as innovative entrepreneurialism or competitiveness. In practice, institutions vacillate between entrepreneurialism and competitiveness; or perhaps entrepreneurialism and competitiveness do not exist as separate categories but more on a continuum. Many organizations combine elements of entrepreneurialism and competitiveness. Whatever the case, innovation is the central ingredient that underlies organizational success. The question arises, then, as to what underlies innovation. Are there certain characteristics that enable an organization to innovate?

Creativity is a necessary innovation component, but it does not guarantee innovation. Innovation requires change, and change requires action. In turn, action requires effective planning. Writers have long spoken of the need to take risks and continually engage in efforts to reinvent one's organization whereby new innovations replace old ones over time. Foster (1986) drew on his vast experience as a consultant and wrote of the need to break from past innovation and purposefully create discontinuities so that you constantly reinvent yourself and "stay ahead of the curve." Organizational development theorists have emphasized the need to foster a welcoming environment and cultural infrastructure that support the creativity, risk taking, and action necessary to innovate and change (Gallos, 2006). Several authors attempt to tie the characteristics of innovation to its results suggesting that organizations that innovate possess clear goals. In doing so they accomplish one or more of the following: create new markets, extend offerings, reduce costs and conserve resources, improve production or delivery processes, and/or engage in socially and environmentally responsible behavior (Amabile, 1996; Davila, Epstein, & Shelton, 2006; Luecke & Katz, 2003).

All of the colleges and universities in this chapter, whether they sought out new possibilities or combined existing resources in new and exciting ways, share a number of characteristics: a creative spirit, a bias for action, an ability to plan effectively, a commitment to goals, a healthy respect for risk taking, a willingness to commit to and an understanding of the amount of time change takes, a supportive culture, and well-defined reasons for engaging in change. Just as importantly, the colleges and universities we highlight in this chapter provide examples of how strategy and innovation overlap. These institutions drew on the strategies described throughout this book, or variations of them.

Lane Community College and Cape Cod Community are institutions that are passionate about the environment. Lane is committed to conservation; Cape Cod focuses on environmental sustainability. Both institutions improved operational efficiencies while moving toward conservation and sustainability. They also capitalized on those efforts in ways that differentiated their programs. Lane and Cape Cod translated their environmental commitments and institutional actions directly into their existing programs. In chapter 6, we state that the crux of differentiation is uniqueness. Existing programs at the colleges took on an added dimension when conservation and sustainability principles were integrated into them, thus providing a degree of differentiation that today allows them to compete for students and resources.

Evergreen State College is a modern day case study in planning and execution. The origin of this institution rests on the interdisciplinary concept envisioned (and brought to fruition) by its founders. The principles of strategic planning certainly paved the way for the institution's success, and the entire concept of the college would not have worked had the leaders of the school not considered context and industry parameters (Chapters 4 and 5). The most interesting aspect of Evergreen's story, from a strategy perspective, however, lies in the implementation of the interdisciplinary concept across different themes. At its core, strategy canvassing is about taking the relevant components and ideas from different arenas and combining them to build a new creation. That is entrepreneurial innovation at its finest. The very notion that someone at the institution thought about how best to create a holistic experience that might help students relate to the broader social and cultural infrastructure of their worlds perhaps seems heady and unrealistic. By drawing on curriculum from music, cultural studies, leadership, and sailing, the institution selected relevant elements from these disciplines and combined them in a way that creates a new educational service for students. Chapter 8 on strategy canvassing provides the systematic tools that one might use to synthesize existing elements into such a new offering. Evergreen created its interdisciplinary synthesis without the aid of a systematic tool, but the concepts of canvassing were clearly at play here. Evergreen's ongoing commitment to its original goals is deserving of special note as well. In its forty-some years, Evergreen has never wavered in its commitment to interdisciplinary education. It has fine-tuned its approach and experimented with different combinations, but it continues to promote interdisciplinary learning to this day.

Planning time and having time to perfect and practice innovative behaviors vary depending on the magnitude of the change. More far-reaching shifts require more deliberate analysis and an awareness of one's organization and industry parameters. Colorado State University spent three years planning its Superclusters. The university also took a risk, albeit a calculated one. In fact, CSU undertook what its leadership refers to as responsible risk. True, Superclusters could fail to work as predicted. They could become bogged down in bureaucratic red tape and could devolve into spats between faculty and business personnel, but CSU sees the upside—quicker dissemination of research findings—as worth the risk they took in restructuring operations.

CSU is also working to provide a supportive culture for the teams that populate the Superclusters. The very idea of creating a team of scientists and business experts who simultaneously provide their expertise while pursuing the goals of the team pushes the ideas of integration (Chapter 7) further than ever before. In a classic sense, vertical integration is functionally very linear: the university does research, patents the research, tests for marketability, then commercializes and sells it. CSU's Superclusters may well popularize a new strategy that we might call simultaneous integration, whereby all the functions and professionals who produce the functions work together in real time, simultaneously, to reach the end goal of getting a research idea from the lab to the market in a more timely fashion. In the Supercluster world, integration cannot be linear because it takes too much time; the simultaneous function of the previously vertically integrated team means more cross-pollination of ideas and enhanced communication flow among team members throughout the entire process. Perhaps the best way to think about CSU's entrepreneurialism is to think of the creation of the Superclusters as a new innovation that does not yet have an established name or technique. It might be that the process by which the Superclusters have been created is itself an innovation from which others can learn.

CAN WE BE INNOVATIVE?

Throughout this chapter, the evidence from the higher education examples suggests that engaging in innovative behaviors does not mean taking reckless and irresponsible risks. It does not mean that colleges and universities abandon planning, industry analysis, or using strategies, such as cost leadership, differentiation, focus, or vertical and horizontal integration. It does mean seeing possibilities that others miss and acting on well-reasoned options in a timely manner. It means having facility with numerous strategy tools and periodically asking general questions:

1. Are we, as an organization, open to new ideas?
2. Are we willing to act?
3. Can we plan effectively?
4. Are we willing to take reasonable risks?
5. Does our institution's culture support innovation?

A KEY TO EFFECTIVE STRATEGY MAKING

The one ingredient to effective strategy we have not talked about is leadership. Degraff and Quinn (2007) outline seven steps for leading innovation: synthesize, strategize, socialize, supervise, synchronize, specialize, and systemize. The first two steps that Degraff and Quinn identify have much to do with assessing one's own organization and establishing purpose and vision. From a strategy standpoint, the value of Chapters 2 and 3 in this book is that strategic planning has indeed provided a systematic framework by which organizational leaders can accomplish Degraff and Quinn's initial steps. The remaining seven steps deal with mobilizing and leading a team through the process of reaching distinct goals.

Leadership has been acknowledged as an essential factor in change, organizational culture, and strategy. In fact, Schein (1992) considers leadership and culture two sides of the same coin. Culture is certainly the carrier of organizational communication, but it is strategy that moves people to action. Leaders within an organization are responsible for building the collective capacity to define and execute a strategy. Indeed, one cannot complete a discussion on strategy without addressing the leadership aspect of it. And the question arises: What strategies must leaders employ to successfully move toward the future? The integral role of leadership in effective strategy making is the subject of the tenth and final chapter.

CHAPTER 10

INNOVATIVE STRATEGY MAKING AND THE ROLE OF LEADERSHIP

New Mexico Institute of Mining and Technology (NMT) began as a School of Mines in 1889. Although the school still offers mining related degrees, today most of its degree programs focus on fields that use mining faculty expertise in unique combinations. NMT now houses one of the foremost hydrology programs in the world. Expertise in physics and geology, which both provide a core knowledge base for mining research, have been combined to produce world-renowned programs in geophysics, geoscience, petroleum recovery, and astro- and atmospheric physics. Its once stellar program in weapons development and testing (which originally filled a national defense need) now positions itself in the growing field of homeland security. Each new degree fills an emerging or anticipated need not readily detected by other mining schools. Tech's forward thinking has converted it from a school of mines into an elite research powerhouse.

Innovative strategy making resembles NMT's movement over time. NMT's mantra has always been about "getting different," a concept very much encouraged by Hamel and Prahalad (1994). Like NMT, smart organizations tailor their strategy making, streamlining and combining strategic planning and competitive strategy into a seamless process that meets unit-specific needs. Above all else, they innovate. Effective strategy makers

---

Innovative Strategy Making in Higher Education, pages 139–150
Copyright © 2009 by Information Age Publishing
139

may concentrate on what already works in the marketplace, what can be improved or expanded, or what is missing. Whatever the case, effective strategists find, pursue, and capitalize on opportunities.

Taking advantage of opportunities left fallow by others is a cornerstone of innovative strategy making and requires consistent guidance from competent leaders. NMT's ability to collectively move forward required presidents, provosts, deans, and department chairs who, over time, helped others identify and capitalize on blips in the environment that were converted into institutional advantages as the university moved into the future.

In chapters 2-9 we mainly addressed strategy from a technical perspective, in the sense of providing concepts and tools that form the very foundation of strategy making. But without effective leadership, the use of any of these tools is doomed to failure. More broadly, successful strategy conception and implementation depends on both leaders and followers. What, then, are some of the characteristics that leaders need to have to be successful strategists?

LEADERSHIP ESSENTIALS

Burns (1978) states that leaders need followers as much as followers need leaders. The leader-follower relationship depends on effective communication (Bass, 1990; Eckel, Hill, Green, & Mallon, 1999; Sashkin & Burke, 1990; Witherspoon, 1997), but that communication starts and ends with the leader. The quality of the message and how it gets communicated determines whether or not leaders create meaning for and with others and motivate them to perform by creating images they understand, accept, and respect (Blake & Mouton, 1968; Witherspoon, 1997).

Good leaders promote an inspiring vision accompanied by a set of clear and consistent goals, which they continually communicate throughout the organization. A key error to leading change is under-communicating the vision (Kotter, 2006). When leaders do communicate effectively, they empower and trust others to take significant roles in refining and adjusting the tactics employed to bring the vision to life. Hearing the vision on a regular basis so that its ideas and the goals that underlie it become embedded within the organizational culture and the minds of its members does not guarantee success, but not hearing it almost always results in failure.

Information comes in different forms, and can be communicated in multiple ways. Some information is best communicated face-to-face, while memos and emails may be more effective and efficient for other types of information. There is information that is best conveyed at the department or college level, while other information is best delivered to the entire institution at one event. Throughout the entire process of crafting strategy and stimulating innovation, effective leaders gauge the situation and assess which information is best shared through which channels. Ineffective leaders only use those communication channels with which they are most comfortable, ignoring the situation and appropriateness of the channel. The proper dissemination of information helps organizational members understand the need for innovation, create the process for it, and, ultimately, produce the desired results (Hamel, 2007). In order to produce the desired results, timelines, targets, and measures of progress must be real and accurate, reflecting the actual performance of individuals and organizational units.

Communication is perhaps more critical within the context of strategy making than it is for any other activity that a leader undertakes. Strategy implies action and change. People must collectively define or buy into the strategy because they will be called upon to alter previous patterns of behavior in an effort to create and innovate. Strategic change involves some degree of psychological risk at the individual level and economic risk at the organizational level. Risk implies that failure is a part of innovation, and, in fact, it is. The manner in which leaders manage that failure is often the true test of leadership. Some failures emanate from sources external to the organization and lie outside its span of control. Many, however, originate internally. O'Sullivan (2002) suggests that all organizations, at one time or another, experience internal innovation failure brought on by either a weakness in what he calls the cultural infrastructure or some inadequacy in the innovation process itself. Infrastructure failures result from poor organization, insufficient communication, lack of empowerment, or ineffective knowledge management. Failures within the innovation process occur most frequently because of unclear goal definition, misalignment of action and goals, lack of broad-based participation, little monitoring or evaluation of results, or inconsistent communication and access to information. Whether an internal failure originated within the organization's culture or within the process itself, each of the causes of failure can be eliminated or at least minimized by effective leadership communication.

LEADERSHIP WITHIN THE HIGHER EDUCATION CONTEXT

Higher education is a knowledge industry, and the faculty who supply the primary labor for institutional functionality are highly educated, often inwardly driven, and frequently skeptical of anybody's ideas but their own or those of a few close colleagues. Successful innovation depends on focused, purposeful work that not only benefits individuals but the institution as a whole—and this is especially true for organizations whose primary labor force share the characteristics of faculty. Colleges and universities confront a special challenge when they attempt to encourage faculty to contribute to a coordinated and collective effort because faculty productivity is in large part recognized and rewarded by experts and associations outside the institution's walls. Similarly, faculty loyalty and the sense of affiliation often lie with professional academic communities outside the college or university that employs them. Membership in these communities guarantees access to career-building networks and provides a clear sense of whom they are as scholars. Yet, without diligence, persistence, and commitment to the broader institution, the talent, ingenuity, and knowledge housed in colleges and universities goes relatively untapped (Drucker, 2002). It takes an effective leader to engender commitment to the broader institution, especially among a highly educated and independent membership such as faculty.

Goffee and Jones (2007) raised the question: "How do you manage people who don't want to be led and may be smarter than you?" They refer to these individuals as "clever people." Clever people abound in colleges and universities. They are highly intelligent, know their worth, expect to be appreciated, and want to be protected (through tenure), yet demand the freedom to explore and fail. In fact, in failing, they often hit on their greatest discoveries. (Because of a lab blunder, a psychologist from the New Mexico Institute of Mining and Technology, who was trying to determine the cause of nausea in astronauts, discovered the nicotine patch.)

The emerging challenges and issues that colleges and universities face require the collective attention of leaders and the clever people they lead. As much as some faculty would like, these concerns cannot be relegated entirely to the administration. Because the knowledge faculty possess is individual, not institution-specific, the challenge for leaders (administrators) is to create environments in which clever people can thrive and to which they become strongly committed. The commitment must translate into a willingness to help tackle matters as they pertain to institutional vitality and the good of the whole.

No matter where in the institution a leader functions—president, provost, vice president, dean, department chair, or coordinator—clever people expect intellectual contemporaries who engage in straightforward dialogue. Faculty do not see themselves ensconced in traditional supervisor-subordination relationships. They ignore rules they consider unfair, punitive, or irrelevant and respond badly to insincerity. Ironically, even though faculty might ignore most bureaucratic trappings and rebel against control, the larger a college or university the greater the inclination for its leaders to become top-down, autocratic, and uniform in their approach to accomplishing the work of the institution.

Because colleges and universities face competitive challenges that will very likely require change, the most productive solutions will arise from combined efforts guided by leaders that emerge at multiple institutional levels. Someone must champion the change, others must actually lead the work of change, and still others must collaborate to bring about the change (Wolverton, 1998). Leaders have the power to champion the process. They must commit human and fiscal resources for a sustained period, guarantee that an adaptive organizational climate exists, and be active in the change but delegate authority to get the work done. Through this all, higher education leaders must continually communicate, at all levels of the organization, for any strategic change to fully take hold. One of the consistent premises in the field of organizational development is that change must be managed and supported from the top-down. This does not mean that leaders must participate in the same activities as others, but it does mean they must have knowledge of and commitment to the change and support the methods to achieve it (Beckhard, 2006).

LEADERSHIP AND STRATEGY MAKING IN ACTION

The remainder of the chapter presents three examples of effective leadership and strategy in higher education, across different types of institutions and at different levels. Bob McCabe presided as president of Miami-Dade College during a period of much change and growth, transforming the institution into a national model for community colleges. Many innovative practices that originated at Miami-Dade are now common practice across the industry. McCabe's changes were so revolutionary that he relied on leadership at all levels of the college to accomplish his vision. Mardee Jenrette directed a major reform initiative at Miami-Dade, and her work demonstrates the power of aligning leadership at all levels of an institution. Lattie Coor, who was the president of Arizona State University throughout the 1990s, led the path that transformed the institution into a formidable research powerhouse. Coor was able to draw on the capacity of his faculty and take advantage of the dynamic geographical context in which ASU resides to reach the research goals that so many constituents desired for the institution. Tad Perry is the executive director of the South Dakota University System, overseeing six universities and the presidents who run them. Perry's leadership is marked by his ability to involve multiple stakeholders, at all levels, in strategic changes, in the face of environmental uncertainty. In each of the three cases, the leaders presided over strategic changes and effectively dealt with those changes. The purpose of the three cases is not so much to focus on the mechanics and tools of strategy but to highlight the role that leaders play in paving the way to success for the strategic changes they champion.

Miami-Dade College

For more than twenty years, Bob McCabe served Miami-Dade Community College (now Miami-Dade College) as executive vice president (ten years) and president (for almost fifteen). Under his leadership, the college engaged in what it termed waves of change, stimulated by innovative ideas that originated with McCabe. The first wave addressed student issues. The college developed a computerized self-advising and registration program that later became the model for other institutions. The college instituted one of the first multicultural curricula in the country, an assessment system for all entering students, and courses that improved the likelihood of their success in college, all of which today are commonplace on many campuses. These changes brought Miami-Dade to national prominence as a community college exemplar. The primary driver behind first-wave changes was the Executive Council, spearheaded by McCabe and comprising upper-level administrators and faculty senate leaders.

McCabe constantly introduced new ideas and was not content to ride the waves of past success. He also understood that student-centered reforms could only do so much and that faculty composition, attitudes, actions, and teaching styles played a crucial role in determining the success or failure of students. McCabe presided over an initiative called the Teaching/Learning Project, which focused on more fundamental organizational changes. The initiative also tapped leadership at all levels of the organization, as faculty and administrators throughout the college were involved in the project. Originally, the project was designed to promote faculty development and tie that development directly to faculty advancement. It involved the creation of an elaborate evaluation process based on portfolio analysis, faculty review, learning centers for faculty, and the establishment of 100 internal endowed chairs for which McCabe personally raised a $7.5 million endowment. In the end, the project developed similar systems for classified staff and administrators.

The project involved turning leadership over to rank-and-file faculty and staff. Although McCabe attended all steering committee meetings, the committee itself consisted of two-thirds faculty (later one-third when staff was included) and one-third top and mid-level administrators. McCabe's role was to explain his ideas and secure the resources needed. McCabe, whether consciously or unconsciously, abided by the sound leadership principles of supporting the work and voicing his commitment to it (Beckhard, 2006), while allowing others to embark on the actions that would bring it to fruition. Mardee Jenrette, a faculty member from Miami-Dade's North campus, headed the steering committee as project director. Steering committee members rotated on and off with more than 500 full-time faculty and staff serving on planning and implementation committees over the project's 10 year life.

Jenrette rose to the leadership challenge when she accepted the directorship of the Teaching/Learning Project. She and the steering committee began by determining what underlying institutional assumptions existed and how they might positively or negatively impact the ultimate goals of the project. They then developed a statement of institutional values, which was vetted by and voted on by Miami-Dade's faculty. Only then did the committee develop a series of subcommittees and task forces that reached out to faculty and later staff. In addition to determining core values, subcommittees reached consensus on the basic characteristics that define faculty, staff, and administrator excellence, established guidelines for hiring and integrating new personnel into the college's system, and examined ways in which support staff and academic leaders could improve the teaching/learning environment. Fourteen subgroups set up criteria for faculty, staff, and administrator evaluation; they designed professional development systems that helped employees meet these criteria; and they developed, implemented, evaluated, revised, and monitored the system. By 1995, the original goals of the project had been expanded, realized, and, for the most part, become a part of how Miami-Dade operated (Wolverton, 1996).

Miami-Dade is really a case study of how change agents implemented strategic change that was championed from the top down. Change agents take their cues from their leaders, whom the literature often refers to as change champions. The change agents who carry out the work of strategic initiatives invoke the capabilities of the socio-technical systems that are needed to implement change. Some change agents are called collaborators because of their exhaustive work and intense commitment to the change. Collaborators are advocates of change, allies of the champion, and supporters of the agenda. They disseminate information about change; identify and recruit people to get involved in the change process; and provide leadership in planning, implementation, monitoring, and review. They come in two stripes (Wolverton, 1998): commissioned (those in titled positions, such as deans and department chairs) and corporal (faculty and staff leaders). Together, they do the hard work of change. McCabe was quite effective at winning collaborators and creating a sense of ownership among them for the various changes he championed.

Arizona State University

Lattie Coor led Arizona State University (ASU) for twelve years. Coor's tenure at ASU demonstrates, perhaps as well as any other example, the payoff to effective planning that is guided by an unwavering vision. Under

Coors's leadership, ASU strategically positioned itself and drew upon many of the tools that we have described throughout this book. Coor set goals, based on a vision of reaching premier research status, and provided faculty and staff with the resources to achieve the necessary goals. But Coor also fostered institutional growth in other ways. For example, he encouraged colleges, departments, and programs to establish relationships with other institutions, such as community colleges—in effect, an integration strategy (influencing and controlling inputs) that increased ASU's diverse student population and at the same time enhanced access for state residents to a growing university.

Coor arrived at ASU in 1990 charged with enthusiasm for what he termed "extraordinary opportunity." This opportunity presented itself when state funding was in question. Many of ASU's students were nontraditional, and though the university was a research institution, it had stalled in its progress toward reaching premier research status.

In his inaugural address, Coor outlined four pillars that would undergird ASU's future. During his tenure, he kept the institution focused on undergraduate education, graduate education and research, cultural diversity, and economic development. During Coor's tenure, the university opened three new campuses, obtained Research 1 status, and brought the Institute of Human Origins from Berkeley to ASU's main campus. Under Coor's guidance, ASU established the Arizona Biomedical Institute; finished a funding campaign raising $560 million, almost twice the original goal; greatly increased the cultural diversity of faculty and students, and became one of the nation's top choices for National Merit scholars.

Coor drew people toward the ideas and actions that he thought were important. He involved them, and they responded to the trust he showed in them. Deans under him had extraordinary authority and responsibility. Deans of ASU's larger colleges controlled more substantial budgets than those of some universities. Deans steadfastly worked to better not only their colleges but the entire institution, engaging faculty in university citizenry and community outreach. Deans became enthusiastic change agents for the president, and their involvement and commitment created a credibility that an individual leader of a substantial organization cannot single-handedly generate. Kotter (2006) states that at least 75% of one's leadership team must be "bought into" a strategic change to have any chance at success; Coor seemed to gain near unanimous buy-in.

Coor never wavered from his belief in the importance of ASU to the state's future, and he raised community awareness and appreciation for ASU's past, present, and future. Coor was a tireless communicator to internal and external stakeholders. In return, the community became a partner in guaranteeing ASU's well being. He had an uncanny sense of timing and took calculated risks as he promoted ASU, garnering support from the

Phoenix business community, which lobbied for and gained funding increases for the university when the state legislature moved to reduce funding in the mid 1990s.

Lattie Coor affected the heart of the university in positive ways. On any measure, from student success to research productivity, ASU got measurably better under Coor. Even more important, the character of the institution changed in positive ways. A sense of stewardship grew, as did the collective pride in its accomplishments. People felt they were part of a team that was building community and contributing to the public good. There was broad ownership in the university's direction, and people found that ASU was a great place to work, while students found it an exciting place to experience their college years.

Throughout his presidency, Coor declared, "I love what I do." He was described as socially responsible yet fiscally conservation, extremely modest yet confident at the same time. One might call him a cautionary entrepreneur. Throughout his twelve years, Coor engaged in innovative thinking, creative strategy, and purposeful action to realize his vision for ASU.

South Dakota University System

The challenges for four-year universities in South Dakota are tied to both economic shifts and demographic realities. South Dakota's overall population growth rate is small, and its young adult population is actually in decline. Many prominent business leaders tenuously hold on to the state's historical ties to agriculture, even as it becomes a smaller part of national and state gross product. From a broad leadership perspective, there are many challenges for higher education in South Dakota.

Within the six-institution university system, structured dialogues between higher education and state leaders have resulted in a purposeful framework on which to base higher education policy and address the many challenges of the state (Martinez, 1999). The dialogues, commonly referred to in the state as roundtables, have occurred in earnest since 1995 and directly aim to set statewide policy priorities for the university system. Tad Perry, the executive director for the South Dakota University System Board of Regents, presided over the initial implementation of the roundtables. Perry used and continues to use the roundtables as a tool to set policy priorities that change practice: shifting away from enrollment driven formulas, using incentive funding, establishing centers of excellence at the various institutions, maintaining and even increasing enrollment amidst demographic challenges, and improving collaboration between faculty and institutions.

In 1995, Perry began working, through the roundtables and other communication vehicles, to set an agenda for higher education, with buy-in from influential politicians, business owners, administrators, and faculty. Perry and his staff have worked for over a decade to talk about higher education at every available opportunity. The ongoing communications from Perry's office reinforce the results of the roundtables and agreed-upon goals for higher education. Interestingly, any state-level meetings dealing with higher education policy and priorities are arranged by Perry's office. As a leader, Perry arranges the meetings and sets the agenda so that the conversation is purposeful and is at least within the guidelines of Perry's vision for the system. From a leadership perspective, Perry is not only bringing people together, he is setting the conditions that govern the interactions, including the venue, the players, and the major topics for discussion. At the same time, Perry has no hidden agenda, and disagreements and points of contention are encouraged, pursued, and fully vetted.

The culmination of the initial work of the roundtables became manifest in 1997 when state leaders formalized a set of public priorities for higher education, a relative rarity on a state level. The process by which these priorities emerged continues today, with refinements and improvements that allow decision makers to learn from the past while keeping an eye on the future. The five original policy priorities that were tied to incentive funding in 1997 were reduced to three target priorities in 2003. The state has also created new policies to coincide with evolving concerns, such as the 2004 implementation of a merit-based aid program intended to improve incentives for high school graduates to attend college in-state.

The operational actions that accompany the broader strategic goals have been real. Faculty members more actively collaborate on research, and it is common that programs across institutions jointly offer courses to minimize unnecessary duplication. Such collaborations send a powerful message to lawmakers that institutions are willing to work together to make public dollars stretch as far as possible. In addition, presidents are more actively involved in recruitment and retention efforts. Perry himself has traveled to states like California to recruit students to South Dakota, convincing them that they will receive a valuable undergraduate experience and there is a place for them at his institutions.

The principles of strategy populate the many strategic efforts that continue in South Dakota to this day. Each of the six institutions has focused its disciplinary offerings for purposes of differentiation; regent staff continually analyze industry trends and its effects on recruitment, participation, and program offerings; and sound principles of planning (vision, goals, measurement) are now an assumed part of how the system and the institutions that comprise it function. The lesson of South Dakota, though, is that leadership matters. Perry's efforts to push change have consistently resulted in consensus among multiple constituents, around innovative strategies that are contributing to the health of an entire system.

CONCLUSIONS

Effective strategy making in higher education requires effective leadership. Effective leaders must also have effective tools. Strategy tools abound and are readily accessible to higher education leaders. Some of these tools allow institutions to more effectively compete within their existing environments for students, funds, donations, and research grants. Other tools can help institutions reshape the very environment in which they live, creating new market space and drawing new customers. We have seen that the various strategy tools or the concepts that define them can be used independently or in combination. The most effective leaders will draw on multiple strategy tools and concepts to create a comprehensive, innovative strategy.

Chapters 2–8 provided a view into the most publicized and well-documented strategy tools available, but in Chapter 9 we acknowledge that the innovative creations of strategy are ever evolving. New tools and methods will surely continue to surface on the strategy scene. On occasion, institutions will even develop innovative strategies that are not easily defined, making it impossible to document systematic steps that others can repeat in search of their own breakthrough ideas. Strategy must have a foundation upon which to build, however, and the strategy tools in this book provide a basis by which sound strategy making can proceed in an ever evolving global postsecondary education and training industry.

Although the emphasis throughout the book is squarely on strategy, the keystone that brings it all together is, in fact, effective leadership. From conception to implementation, effective strategy requires involvement and leadership at all levels of the organization, but especially at the top. Strategy and the change it induces need a point person who engages in purposeful dreaming—comprehensive, broad, and future-oriented—and then communicates the why, what, and how of any needed change. These leaders personally generate many innovative ideas and radiate the energy (Fisher & Koch, 2004) that is required to carry change efforts through their inevitable peaks and valleys. There should be measurable progress along the way, yet strategic change is not achieved in a matter of months. True change is measured in years, though the activities to move toward it may start immediately. That is why the most successful leaders never lose sight of the change agenda toward which they strive.

We drew on the examples of McCabe, Jenrette, Coor, and Perry simply because their successes are well documented and they exhibited the characteristics leaders need to birth new strategies and champion them to completion. Like McCabe and Coor at the institutional level and Jenrette at the program level, these leaders involve people in change and make sure it becomes an organizational reality. They energize people who are excited about the institution, its work, and its future. They also maintain organizational stability in the face of change-related disruptions. Guided by capable leadership, significant change can even occur across an entire state. Perry brought together institutional and state players to the extent that even the governor and powerful legislators truly felt they were part of the change agenda for higher education.

The leaders that we profiled in this book also understood how to work with and lead "clever people." As one ASU employee put it, "Ninety percent of the faculty approved of Coor's leadership." McCabe's actions garnered similar support. And because both Coor and McCabe worked well with faculty, they managed to vastly improve the quality and character of their institutions. They instilled in faculty, staff, and administrators the belief that they could make a difference. Perry consistently wins the support of his six university presidents because the channels of communication create a respectful and trusting environment in which they operate.

In the end, innovative strategy making and great leadership go hand-in-hand. One does not reach its potential without the other. That was true in the past, it is true today, and it will be true in the future. Those leaders who will take their institutions to new heights will not only be able to touch the hearts and minds of the clever people they lead, but they will also be the ones to draw on the many tools of strategy as they forge toward the future.

REFERENCES

Amabile, T. (1996). *Creativity in context.* New York: Westview Press.

Astin, A. W. (1997, Winter). The changing American college student: Thirty-year trends, 1966–1996. *The Review of Higher Education, 21*(2).

Barney, J. B. (1997). *Gaining and sustaining competitive advantage* (2nd ed.). Reading, MA: Addison-Wesley.

Bass, B. M. (1990). *Bass and Stogdill's handbook of leadership* (3rd ed.). New York: Free Press.

Beckhard, R. (2006). What is organizational development? In J. V. Gallos (Ed.), *Organizational development.* San Francisco: Jossey Bass.

Black, J. (2002). *Dictionary of economics* (p. 167). New York: Oxford University Press.

Blake, R. R., & Mouton, J. S. (1968). *Corporate excellence through grid organization development.* Houston, TX: Gulf Publishing.

Blum, T. C., & Bennett, N. (2004). DuPree College of Management at Georgia Tech: A college positioned for a compelling opportunity. In M. Wolverton & L. E. Penley (Eds.), *Elite MBA programs at public universities: What really makes them tick* (pp. 126–142). Westport, CT: Praeger/Greenwood.

Blumenstyk, G. (2006). Marketing, the for-profit way. *The Chronicle of Higher Education, 53*(15), A20.

Blumenthal, D., Epstein, S., & Maxwell, J. (1986). Commericalizing university research: Lessons from the experience of the Wisconsin Alumni Research Foundation. *New England Journal of Medicine, v*(31), 1621–26.

Boyd, D. (2002). *State spending for higher education in the coming decade.* Boulder, CO: The National Center for Higher Education Management Systems. Retrieved November 2006. http://www.nchems.org/presenta.htm

Bryson, J. M. (1988). *Strategic planning for public and nonprofit organizations.* San Francisco: Jossey-Bass.

Burns, J. M. (1978). *Leadership.* New York: Harper & Row.

Campbell, A., & Alexander, M. (1997, November-December). What's wrong with strategy? *Harvard Business Review,* 42–51.

Innovative Strategy Making in Higher Education, pages 151–155
Copyright © 2009 by Information Age Publishing
All rights of reproduction in any form reserved.

Christensen, C. M. (1997). *The innovator's dilemma: When new technologies cause great firms to fail.* Boston: Harvard Business School Press.

Chronicle of Higher Education Almanac. (2007). Washington, DC: *The Chronicle of Higher Education, 52*(1), 45.

The College Board. (2006). Trends in student aid. *Trends in Higher Education Series* (p. 22). Washington, DC.

Coyne, K. P., Clifford, P. G., & Dye, R. (2007). Breakthrough thinking from inside the box. *Harvard Business Review, 85*(12), 71–83.

Davila, T., Epstein, M. J., & Shelton, R. (2006). *Making innovation work: How to manage it, measure it, and profit from it.* Upper Saddle River, NJ: Wharton School Publishing.

Degraff, J., & Quinn, S.E. (2007). *Leading innovation: How to jump start your organization's growth engine.* New York: McGraw Hill.

Doucette, D., Richardson, R. C., Jr., & Fenske, R. H. (1985, March/April). Defining institutional mission. *Journal of Higher Education, 56*(2).

Drucker, P. F. (2002, August). The discipline of innovation. *Harvard Business Review,* 95–104.

Eckel, P., Hill, B., Green, M., & Mallon, B. (1999). *On change. Reports from the road: Insights on institutional change.* An Occasional Paper Series of the ACE Project on Leadership and Institutional Transformation. Washington, DC: American Council on Education.

Farrell, E. F., & Van Der Werf, M. (2007, May 25). Playing the rankings game. *The Chronicle of Higher Education, LIII*(38), A11.

Fisher, J. L., & Koch, J. V. (2004). *The entrepreneurial president.* Westport, CT: Praeger.

Foster, R. (1986). *Innovation: The attacker's advantage.* New York: Summit Books.

Frank, H. (2004). The Robert H. Smith School of Business at the University of Maryland: Building a technology powerhouse. In M. Wolverton & L. E. Penley (Eds.), *Elite MBA programs at public universities: How a dozen innovative schools are redefining business education.* Westport, CT: Praeger.

Franklin, A. L., Cawley, M., & Kachel, P.O. (1998). Renovations and innovations in program evaluation: The Arizona experience and its potential for more widespread applicability. *Public Productivity & Management Review, 22*(1).

Fratto, G. M., Jones, M. R., & Cassill, N. L. (2006). An investigation of competitive pricing among apparel retailers and brands. *Journal of Fashion Marketing and Management, 10*(4), 387–404.

Galbraith, J. R., Lawler, E. E. & Associates (1993). *Organizing for the future.* San Francisco: Jossey-Bass.

Gallos, J. V. (Ed.). (2006). *Organizational development.* San Francisco: Jossey Bass.

Geiger, R. (2004). *Money and knowledge: Research universities and the paradox of the marketplace.* Stanford, CA: Stanford University Press.

Gilbert, D. (2006). *Stumbling on happiness.* New York: Alfred Knopf.

Gilley, J. W., Fulmer, K. A., & Reithlingshoefer, S. J. (1986). *Searching for academic excellence.* New York: MacMillan.

Gladieux, L. E., King, J. E., & Corrigan, M. E. (2005). The federal government and higher education. In P. Altbach, O. Berdahl, & P. Gumport (Eds.), *American higher education in the twenty-first century: Social, political, and economic challenges* (2nd ed.). Baltimore, MD: The Johns Hopkins University Press.

Goffee, R., & Jones, G. (2007, March). Leading clever people. *Harvard Business Review, 85*(3), 72–79.

Grant, R. M. (1998). *Contemporary strategy analysis* (3rd ed.). Malden, MA: Blackwell Publishing.

Grant, R. M. (2005). *Contemporary strategy analysis* (5th ed.). Malden, MA: Blackwell Publishing.

Gupta, Y. (2004). A work in progress: Transforming the University of Washington Business School. In M.Wolverton & L. E. Penley (Eds.), *Elite MBA programs at public universities: How a dozen innovative schools are redefining business education.* Westport, CT: Praeger.

Hamel, G. (2007). *The future of management.* Boston: Harvard Business School Press.

Hamel, G., & Prahalad, C. K. (1994). *Competing for the future: Breakthrough strategies for seizing control of your industry and creating the markets of tomorrow.* Boston: Harvard Business School Press.

Hauptman, A. (1997). Financing American higher education. *New directions for institutional research.* San Francisco: Jossey-Bass.

Hope, J., & Fraser, R. (2003). *Beyond budgeting: How managers can break free from the annual performance trap* (p. 6). Boston: Harvard Business School Press.

Hovey, H. (1999). *State spending for higher education in the next decade: The battle to sustain current support.* San Jose, CA: The National Center for Public Policy and Higher Education.

Hunt, M. (1972). *Competition in the major home appliance industry.* Doctoral dissertation, Harvard University.

Ireland, R. D., & Hitt, M. A. (1992, May-June). Mission statements: Importance, challenge, and recommendations for development. *Business Horizons,* 34–42.

Jelinek, M. (1979). *Institutionalizing innovation: A study of organizational learning systems.* New York: Praeger.

Keller, G. (1983). *Academic strategy: The management revolution in American higher education.* Baltimore, MD: Johns Hopkins University Press.

Kim, C.W., & Mauborgne, R. (2005). *Blue ocean strategy.* Boston: Harvard Business School Press.

Kotter, J. (2006). Leading change: Why transformation efforts fail. In J. V. Gallos (Ed.), *Organizational development.* San Francisco: Jossey-Bass.

Kotter, J. P., & Heskett, J. L. (1992). *Corporate culture and performance.* New York: The Free Press.

Lawler, E. (2006). Business strategy: Creating the winning formula. In J. V. Gallos (Ed.), *Organizational development.* San Francisco: Jossey-Bass.

Luecke, R., & Katz, R. (2003). *Mannaging creativity and innovation.* Boston, MA: Harvard Business School Press.

Martinez, M. (1999). *South Dakota: Developing policy-driven change in higher education.* San Jose, CA: The National Center for Public Policy and Higher Education.

Martinez, M. (2004). *Postsecondary participation and state policy* (p. 10). Sterling, VA: Stylus.

McFarland, K. R. (2008). *The breakthrough company: How everyday companies become extraordinary performers.* New York: Crown Business.

McKillips, G. W. with Mullen, R. (2004). J. Mack Robinson College of Business: Reinventing business education in the 21st century. In M. Wolverton & L. E. Penley (Eds.), *Elite MBA programs at public universities: What really makes them tick* (pp. 134–167). Westport, CT: Praeger/Greenwood.

Mintzberg, H. (1989). *Mintzberg on management: Inside our strange world of organizations.* New York: Free Press.

Mintzberg, H. (1994). *The rise and fall of strategic planning.* New York: Free Press.

Mintzberg, H., Ahlstrand, B., & Lampel, J. (1998). *Strategy safari: A guided tour through the wilds of strategic management.* New York: The Free Press.

Morgan, G. (2006). *Images of organizations.* Thousand Oaks, CA: Sage Publications.

Mulchanow, K. (2005). *P-12 and higher education: Areas for coordination and collaboration.* Retrieved December 29, 2005. http://www.unlv.edu/projects/bhes/toolbox/Molchanow_PK–12_collaborations.pdf

New Mexico State University: www.nmsu.edu/about.html, retrieved January 31, 2008.

O'Sullivan, D. (2002). Framework for managing business development in the networked organisation. *Journal of Computers in Industry, 47*(1), 77–88.

Penn, M. J. (2007). *Microtrends: the small forces behind tomorrow's big changes.* New, York: Twelve.

Peterson, M. (1980). *Improving academic management.* San Francisco: Jossey-Bass.

Peterson, M., & Dill, D. (1997). Understanding the postsecondary knowledge industry. In M. Peterson, D. Dill, L. Mets, & Associates (Eds.), *Planning and management for a changing environment.* San Francisco: Jossey-Bass.

Peterson, M., Dill, D. Mets, L. & Associates (Eds.). (1997). *Planning and management for a changing environment.* San Francisco: Jossey-Bass.

Pfeffer, J., & Sutton, R. I. (2006). *Hard facts, dangerous half-truths & total nonsense: Profiting from evidence-based management.* Boston: Harvard Business School Press.

Pines, J., & Gilmore, J. (1999). *The experience economy: Work is theatre and every business a stage.* Boston: Harvard Business School Press.

Pines, J. M. (2006). The economic role of the emergency medical department in health care continuum: Applying Michael Porter's five forces model to emergency medicine. *The Journal of Emergency Medicine, 30*(4), 447–453.

Porter, M. E. (1980). *Competitive strategy: Techniques for analyzing industries and competitors.* New York: Free Press.

Porter, M. (1985). *Competitive advantage: Creating and sustaining superior performance.* New York: Free Press.

Quinn, J. B., Mintzberg, H., & James, R. M. (1988). *Strategic process.* Englewood Cliffs, NJ: Prentice-Hall.

Roberto, M. A. (2002). *Robert Modavi & the wine industry.* Cambridge, MA: Harvard Business School Publishing. HBS Case # 9-302-102.

Rowley, D. J., Lujan, H. D., Dolence, M. G. (1997). *Strategic change in colleges and universities: Planning to survive and prosper.* San Francisco: Jossey-Bass.

Sashkin, M., & Burke, W. W. (1990). Understanding and assessing organizational leadership. In K. E. Clark & M. B. Clark (Eds.), *Measures of leadership* (pp. 297–325). West Orange, NJ: Leadership Library of America.

Schein, E. H. (1992). *Organizational culture and leadership* (2nd ed.). San Francisco: Jossey-Bass.

Shirley, R. C. (1988, Winter). Strategic planning: An overview. In D. W. Steeples (Ed.), *New directions for higher education*. San Francisco: Jossey-Bass.

Slaughter, S. & Leslie, L. L. (1997). *Academic capitalism: Politics, policies, and the entrepreneurial university*. Baltimore, MD: Johns Hopkins University Press.

Tapscott, D., & Williams A. D. (2006). *Wikinomics: How mass collaboration changes everything*. New York: Portfolio.

Taylor, B. E., & Massey, W. F. (1996). *Strategic indicators for higher education: Vital benchmarks and information to help you evaluate and improve your institution's performance*. Princeton, NJ: Peterson's.

Trombley, W. (1998). Performance based budgeting. *CrossTalk, 6*(1). San Jose, CA: The National Center for Public Policy and Higher Education.

Weisbord, M. R. (1996). Transforming teamwork: Work relationships in a fast-changing world. In S. Ott, *Classic readings in organizational behavior* (2nd ed.). Belmont, CA: Wadsworth.

Welch, J., & Welch, S. (2005). *Winning*. New York: HarperBusiness.

Witherspoon, P. D. (1997). *Communicating leadership: An organizational perspective*. Boston: Allyn and Bacon.

Wolverton, M. (1996, Fall). Planning and pain in Miami. *Planning for Higher Education, 25*(1), 14–19.

Wolverton, M. (2006). Three Georgias in Atlanta: Lessons from business schools about finding your identity. *International Journal of Educational Management, 20*(7), 507–519.

Wolverton, M. (1998). Champions, agents and collaborators: leadership keys to successful systemic change. *Journal of Higher Education Policy and Management, 20*(1), 19–30.

Wolverton. M., & Penley, L. E. (Eds.). (2004). *Elite MBA programs at public universities: How a dozen innovative schools are redefining business education*. Westport, CT: Praeger.

Ziegenfuss, J. T., Jr. (1989). *Designing organizational futures: A systems approach to strategic planning with cases for public and non-profit organizations*. Springfield, IL: Charels C. Thomas.

ABOUT THE AUTHORS

Mario C. Martinez is associate professor of higher education at the University of Nevada, Las Vegas. His writing focuses on competencies, strategy, and higher education policy. Mario has been training and consulting on topics related to human systems and human interaction for over ten years, and prior to becoming a professor he worked in private industry and state government.

Mimi Wolverton is a retired professor of higher education who writes about leadership and strategy and consults with universities on faculty leadership development and program design. She holds an MBA and a Ph.D. from Arizona State University and spent more than twenty years in industry and twelve years teaching at universities in the western United States.

INDEX

A

Action Plan, 43
Action Statements, 43–44
Ahlstrand, B., 107
Albuquerque, New Mexico, 79
Amabile, T., 134
American Bar Association, 56
American Management Association, 46
Anglicans, 111
Apple, Inc., 129–130
Arizona Biomedical Institute, 146
Arizona State College, 34
Arizona State University, 34, 56, 76,
    143, 145, 157
Arizona, 20, 52, 56, 78
Articulation, 77, 93, 95, 99, 105
Astin, A., 55
Atlanta, Georgia, 80, 122,

B

Backward Integration, 92–95, 99, 105
Baptists, 111
Bargaining Power of Buyers, 47–48,
    56–59, 66, 70–71
Bargaining Power of Suppliers, 47–48,
    58–59, 71

Barney, J. B., 78, 80
Bass, B. M., 140,
Bayh–Dole Act, The, 97
Baylor University, 57
Bennett, N., 80
Blue Ocean Creation, 108
Blum, T. C., 80
Blumenstyk, G., 151
Blumenthal, D., 97
Boston Consulting Group, x
Boston, Massachusetts, 87
Boyd, D., 16
Brown University, 111
Burke, W. W., 140
Burns, J. M., 140

C

California State System, 126
California State University, Los Angeles,
    76
California State University, Monterey
    Bay, 126
Cape and Islands Renewable Collabora-
    tive, 131
Cape Cod Community College, 131, 135
Capella University, 50
Capital Requirements, 48–50, 67–68

Innovative Strategy Making in Higher Education, pages 159–165
Copyright © 2009 by Information Age Publishing
159

CPSIA information can be obtained at www.ICGtesting.com
Printed in the USA
LVOW07s1016140913

352433LV00005B/51/P